D0629991

Praise for *The Relationship Engine*

"Ed Wallace provides a critical reminder that for successful business relationships we must clearly demonstrate our value proposition and cut through increasingly complex challenges by remembering the power of 1 to 1 relationships to get things done. *The Relationship Engine* provides actionable insight into the art and science of being a relational leader and helps you transform your 'Colleague' relationships into 'Advocates.'"

—Kristin M. Risi, assistant dean, Corporate Relations and Executive Education, LeBow College of Business, Drexel University

"*The Relationship Engine* provides compelling thinking about the impact of strong business relationships. The great news is that Ed Wallace actually walks us through how to launch new relationships and turn them into advocates."

—Jennifer DeMello-Johnson, AVP, Amerisure Insurance Company

"In *The Relationship Engine*, Ed Wallace shares advanced insights into the power of business relationships and how this underutilized asset is the key to the meaningful achievement of any organization's mission. I recommend this book to everyone from C- Suite to shop floor."

—Jeff Westphal, CEO, Vertex Inc.

"If you're in business, you're in the people business – and the people business is about relationships, whether internal or external. This book is a great tool for leaders at all levels to apply their relationship skills."

—Tom Feeney, president and CEO, Safelite AutoGlass

"Whatever our professional endeavors, our success in large part rests on the success of our relationships. Are we properly communicating with our coworkers? Are we inspiring each other to do great work? There is a connection between the status of our relationships and said greatness. In *The Relationship Engine*, Ed Wallace shows detailed examples of these connections and how to make every interaction matter."

—Michael Barkann, Comcast/NBC sports anchor

"The Principle of Making Every Interaction Matter that Ed so eloquently lays out is one that should resonate with every business leader who reads this book. Practice it daily!"

—William R. Carteaux, president and CEO, Plastics Industry Association

"Ed Wallace's Principle of Worthy Intent is a simple yet powerful approach to building lasting trust and productive relationships in the workplace.
—Chris Malone, co-author of *The HUMAN Brand: How We Relate to People, Products and Companies*

"Ed Wallace has been championing Relational Capital for years, helping individuals and organizations be more effective with amazing results. With his new book, Ed directs his purpose towards leadership with astonishing clarity and accessibility. The New Value Prop for leaders is timely, needed, and an irrefutable must-read, both simple and powerful . . . to help build and sustain leadership."
—David Henkin, author of *Conversation Innovation: A Corporate Fable on Leadership Coaching and the Power of Conversations*

"In an age where all business is global, with new competitors and new ways of doing business opening up constantly, and every product or service being commoditized and reduced to price-based competition, the only way to compete will be through developing relationships that add value and meaning to people and their business. Ed Wallace's book is a breath of fresh air in this otherwise bleak outlook. The principles and ideas outlined in this book are groundbreaking and create more than a competitive advantage. If you are serious about your business and competing well into the future this book is a must read!"
—Corey Sigvaldason, PhD, consultant, trainer, speaker, author, coach

"Nobody cares what you know until they know that you care. Ed Wallace shows you how to be the best person you can be in every business setting and sincerely connect. Through his process, relationships are formed and a foundation to transact business is created."
—Jim Reichwein, SVP, Sales and Marketing, Logicalis, Inc.

"I continue to be extremely impressed by Ed Wallace's simple yet powerful messages on the importance of strong business relationships. This book adds tremendous value for its audiences, in particular newer generations entering the business world. Buy it, read it, and apply it to your pipeline of early talent!"
—Eric D. Taylor, director, Global Talent Management, Arthur J. Gallagher and Co.

THE
RELATIONSHIP
ENGINE

THE RELATIONSHIP ENGINE

CONNECTING WITH
THE PEOPLE WHO POWER
YOUR BUSINESS

ED WALLACE

◊AMACOM
American Management Association
New York * Atlanta * Brussels * Chicago * Mexico City * San Francisco
Shanghai * Tokyo * Toronto * Washington, DC

Bulk discounts available. For details visit:
www.amacombooks.org/go/specialsales
Or contact special sales: Phone: 800-250-5308 | Email: specialsls@amanet.org
View all the AMACOM titles at: www.amacombooks.org
American Management Association: www.amanet.org

This publication is designed to provide accurate and authoritative information in regard to the subject matter covered. It is sold with the understanding that the publisher is not engaged in rendering legal, accounting, or other professional service. If legal advice or other expert assistance is required, the services of a competent professional person should be sought.

Library of Congress Cataloging-in-Publication Data

Names: Wallace, Ed, 1959- author.
Title: The relationship engine : connecting with the people who power your
    business / by Ed Wallace.
Description: New York City : AMACOM, 2016.
Identifiers: LCCN 2016024566 | ISBN 9780814437131 (hardcover) | ISBN
    9780814437148 (ebook)
Subjects: LCSH: Business communication. | Interpersonal relations. | Business
    networks. | Success in business.
Classification: LCC HF5718 .W35 2016 | DDC 650.1/3--dc23 LC record available at
    https://lccn.loc.gov/2016024566

ABOUT AMA
American Management Association (www.amanet.org) is a world leader in talent development, advancing the skills of individuals to drive business success. Our mission is to support the goals of individuals and organizations through a complete range of products and services, including classroom and virtual seminars, webcasts, webinars, podcasts, conferences, corporate and government solutions, business books, and research. AMA's approach to improving performance combines experiential learning—learning through doing—with opportunities for ongoing professional growth at every step of one's career journey.

10 9 8 7 6 5 4 3 2

For Laurie, Brett, Grant, Dylan and Hannah,

my all-time great relationships

Success comes through

the experience we create

for others!

Acknowledgments

THIS BOOK WOULD NOT exist if it were not for the incredible Relational Leaders that I have been blessed to know and work with throughout my life. These wonderful human beings are not people who just put words up on the walls of their companies and workstations; they truly live, succeed and help others through the power of Worthy Intent. Like them, I believe that our success in life and business is the sum set of everyone we have known and the experiences we have created and shared together. I am honored to acknowledge them here.

To Connie and Jennifer, your strength and commitment continues to inspire

Lynn DiBonaventura, for your incredible knowledge and friendship

Curtis Skowronek, the most challenging expert on earth

Paul Wesman, you're four for four with "our" books

Chris Malone, you truly understand "the human brand"

Corey Sigvaldason, thank you for your wisdom and support from north of the border

Tom Feeney, Natalie Crede and Melina Metzger, thank you for your Caring Hearts

Jennifer DeMello-Johnson, you are a true force of nature

Bill Carteaux and Jane Mott-Palmer, thank you for helping me understand the true beauty and value of "plastic"

Cam Hicks and Chris Brady, thank you for your trust

John Romer, Lynn Robinson and Tyler Tuttle, your village continues to grow

Jeff Westphal, Advocate for life

John McLeod, thank you for believing in the Relational Capital concepts

Laura Vaupel, my alter ego from the West Coast, thank you for being such an Advocate

Eric Whipple, Charlie Poznek, Jerry Block, Sue Baker, Dave Pedorenko, and Leslie Fiorilla, my winning team

Frank Coates, thanks for getting right to the point

Lyle Flom and Tim Clark, thank you for investing in our business relationship

Riki Hirsh, thank you for believing that relationships are just as important internationally

Kim Martinez, thank you for your insights into toll takers and, most importantly, the power of business relationships

Dr. Kris Risi, you make me smarter

Frank Contigiani, over thirty years ago you knew what it was all about—relationships

José Palomino, your genius again is evident in this work

John Burns and Matt Burns, who says that engineers can't be funny and smart?

Nicole Morgenstern, thank you for your support with AMACOM

Stephen S. Power, thank you for your expertise with this book

Matt Nestor, thank you for jumping in to make this project a success

Kim and Jason, your hearts and minds continue to help me grow

CONTENTS

PREFACE: The Power of Worthy Intent   xix

INTRODUCTION: The New Value Proposition for Leaders   1

PART I

THE FIVE PRINCIPLES OF THE RELATIONAL LEADER   9

1 The Relationship Paradox   11

2 Principle #1: Display Worthy Intent   31

3 Principle #2: Care about People's Goals, Passions and Struggles   49

4 Principle #3: Make Every Interaction Matter   71

5 Principle #4: Value People Before Processes   81

6 Principle #5: Connect Performance to a Purpose   89

PART I

EXECUTIVE SUMMARY   98

CONTENTS

PART II

RELATIONAL AGILITY: HARNESSING THE POWER OF WORTHY INTENT   101

7   The Relational Agility Process: Navigating the
     Complexity   103

8   Launching Business Relationships with Colleagues   119

9   Advancing Relationships with Professional Peers   137

10   Elevating Relationships with Advocates   151

PART II

EXECUTIVE SUMMARY   161

PART III

BECOMING A RELATIONAL LEADER: A PRACTICAL APPROACH   163

11   Tools for the Relational Leader   165

12   Take the Relational Leader Challenge   177

13   Five Ways to Sustain the Relationships You
     Create   191

     Appendix: Relational Ladder Abstract   197

     Endnotes   203

     Glossary   205

     Index   209

     Other Books by Ed Wallace   217

THE
RELATIONSHIP
ENGINE

PREFACE

The Power of Worthy Intent

ON AUGUST 26, 2005, I got a phone call from my wife, Laurie. She was not her usual calm, collected self and I could sense something had happened. Our young son Grant apparently had fallen off a skateboard at a friend's home, hitting his head on the pavement, and the paramedics were on the way. We agreed to get off the phone so we could concentrate on driving. Within seconds, though, the phone rang again and Laurie, who was an ER nurse, was noticeably upset when she told me that instead we needed to head to the local community college where the helipad was located. The next ten minutes seemed like forever as I felt as though I had absolutely no control over what was occurring. I thought about what Grant must be going through with all of those strangers around him. Was he afraid? Was he even awake? Could he move his legs?

At the community college, I saw the helicopter and ambulance and all the surrounding commotion. I have to tell you, nothing can prepare you for something like this, no matter how many books you read on parenting, leadership or personal development. I ran to the ambulance and found that Grant was awake but in and out of consciousness due to a sedative they had given him. I tried to assure him I was there, but his head was in the blocks and all that I could do was rub his legs to signal my presence. He responded by moving them a bit and I was somewhat reassured.

Laurie arrived with our other son, Brett. She immediately took on her ER nurse role, even while her emotions were eating her alive. She does not like to fly, but she jumped right into the helicopter with Grant. Brett came over and hugged me as we watched them take off.

He's a special needs kid and you can't even imagine how amazing he was during this ordeal.

Brett and I now needed to drive to the hospital, which was forty-five minutes away. I tried to put on a strong front, but we both broke down and just prayed that Grant would be all right.

After a tense drive, we reached the Children's Hospital of Philadelphia (CHOP), one of the largest in the country. Due to construction and traffic, we needed to park in the general parking garage, then rushed into the building and entered a large atrium filled with people and activity. It was a moment when we could have been overcome with anxiety, confusion and fear; we had no idea where to look for Grant and Laurie or whom to ask.

Before these concerns had a chance to form in my mind, representatives from the hospital appeared out of nowhere and asked if we were the family of Grant Wallace. We said we were and they assured us that Grant was stable, and they swiftly proceeded to take us directly to the room where the doctors were caring for him.

It was not until recently that I fully realized just how remarkable this seemingly innocuous experience was. This was one of the top children's hospitals in the country, a large, complex institution, widely acclaimed and trusted for the quality of its medical care. Thousands of children were treated there daily. Even though I, as a parent, felt lost and anxious about finding my son and wife in this urgent moment, the hospital had no particular reason or motivation to go to the trouble to delegate employees to go out *looking* for me just to get us to the room five minutes faster. But the fact that they *did* do this had a profound effect on me. It spoke volumes. It demonstrated that they truly had *all* of our best interests at heart. It put our feelings and concerns at the top of the priority list. They could have just let us fumble around at the admitting or information desks, asking questions, filling out forms, showing our identification and waiting on a bench. Instead, they personally came and found us and tended to our immediate needs by reuniting us with our family. They showed that their intentions toward us were genuine, good. They valued people and relationships before bureaucratic process and busyness.

I didn't know it then, but that moment was the genesis of the idea I now call Worthy Intent—the guiding principle of effective human relationships—which is central to this book and to our success in life and business.

Despite Grant having a severe concussion and some other complications that needed monitoring, the story does have a happy ending. The process eventually took a few months, but he came through with flying colors. Today, he is fine and—as of this writing—is pitching for his college baseball team.

INTRODUCTION

The New Value Proposition for Leaders

THE ROLE OF A leader has evolved. Tom Feeney, president and CEO of Safelite AutoGlass, recently validated that point for me. He stated, "It is no longer enough to merely direct action; today we must inspire and empower belief, which requires us to build more trusting relationships with people than ever before. This applies to leading people within your organization and it applies to becoming a leading brand. Customers no longer buy what you sell; *they buy what you stand for.* Relevant and sustainable brands are those that build love, loyalty and trusting relationships with their customers." Wow, this was the first time I ever heard a CEO use the word "love" in their description of leadership!

Such is the paradigm shift for Safelite's leaders. Their job descriptions now contain phrases like "Think People First" and "Caring Heart" to describe required characteristics and expected interactions with both associates and customers. To date, nearly three-quarters of Safelite's leaders have successfully embraced this leadership "transformation," evidenced (quantitatively and subjectively) by their rapid growth and strengthening business results. Safelite's Relational Leaders strive to become the kind of people who other people enjoy working with and focus on winning every day through the impact they have on other human beings.

I will share more on Tom and Safelite's version of Relational Leadership later in this book along with compelling approaches from leading "people" organizations like Teleflex, DaVita Rx, Southwest Airlines, Plastics Industry Association, and many others. And it isn't just large corporations that have enacted these changes. You will also discover that some of the best Relational Leaders are taking this approach at small businesses, like golf driving ranges and animal rescues.

RELATIONAL LEADERSHIP

What exactly is a Relational Leader? First, this is not an exclusive club for senior executives. Unlike many leadership models that focus on management and high-potential employees, anyone can be a Relational Leader. I have known and continue to marvel at the Relational Leaders I meet at all levels throughout companies, and even a few who are not even in organizations at all. Second, a Relational Leader's value proposition is to create a superior experience for others as the key driver of business performance. That experience can manifest from working on a corporate strategy all the way down to greeting someone who works in the company cafeteria. Finally, Relational Leaders "competitor-proof" their organizations and themselves through a consistent, intentional focus on investing in the relational capital—the distinctive value created by people in a business relationship—needed to drive performance in today's complex, quickly commoditized business environment.

Ultimately, a Relational Leader is anyone who *intentionally* puts the other person's goals and values at the forefront of each business relationship, creating an exceptional experience for others. This principle is known as Worthy Intent and it allows Relational Leaders to create relationships that immunize them against all competitors both within and outside their organizations.

WHAT'S MISSING?

Most executives and managers will tell you that strong human relationships are critical to their success. They say they also need their team members and employees to be great at developing and maintaining relationships, collaborating, innovating, advocating for company goals and keeping the organization functioning effectively. These leaders would say human relationships—as opposed to digital or what I like to call "ethereal" relationships—are central to their ability to influence and inspire individuals to achieve their organization's mission. Whether it's external or internal business relationships, we need to understand how people think and act, what it takes for someone to want to listen to you, help you, work for you, work with you and even buy from you. In fact, with all of the mergers and acquisitions going on in business today, ultimately, it is how people are regarded, valued, treated and communicated to that will determine if the transaction succeeds or fails to deliver its promises. Sadly, most acquisitions fail to meet their intended promises and goals.

Organizations are first and foremost composed of people. All the material factors that undergird a company—patents, intellectual property, real estate, processes, markets, products, services— are useless without harmonious, working relationships among the people involved. Take for instance an intangible asset like a patent. It is basically useless without humans thinking, assessing and assigning a value to it, and then applying it to benefit an individual or group. It is people who have the ideas, who partner and collaborate with each other, who exercise judgment, who foresee the future of the industry, who make connections that spark a new venture, etc. You cannot win new customers or retain old ones without developing and maintaining strong human relationships, and you can't succeed in managing a company that way either.

Very few leaders, however, would say they take any kind of structural, systematic approach to doing this—probably because they are not aware that this is possible. The common result is a haphazard, almost accidental process of relationship development. In other words, they do the best they can with relationships as the opportunities come along and hope for the best.

Now, let's think about what's off about this picture. In any other discipline—music, sports, dance, chemistry, you name it—how are successful results achieved? Each discipline has defining principles, laws or tenets. Only disciplined, persistent adherence to the principles allows for consistent excellence and success.

So what's missing or why are leaders missing the relational mark? My experience through many years of research into business relationships and working with more than twenty thousand professionals and over two hundred fifty companies and organizations has shown me that there are five identifiable principles that lead to effective relationship development and, not surprisingly, superior performance. These don't exist only in the world of business development where most people believe relationships are the most important. They are at the very heart of the practice of the most successful leaders at all levels in organizations and life. Through my experiences and research, I know they can be learned, practiced and improved, bringing a surprising level of precision to relationships in organizations.

The Five Principles
1. Display Worthy Intent
2. Care About People's Goals, Passions and Struggles

3. Make Every Interaction Matter
4. Value People Before Processes
5. Connect Performance to a Purpose

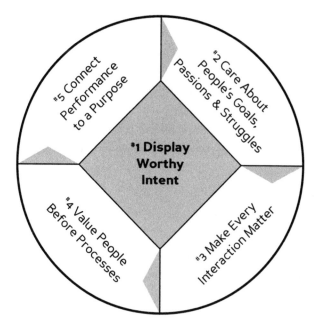

Figure I-1. Relational Leadership.

THE FIVE PRINCIPLES OF THE RELATIONAL LEADER

These principles form a system of beliefs for high performers that Relational Leaders follow and apply intentionally. I define "Intentionality"—represented by the shaded arrows in figure I.1—as the means by which Relational Leaders coordinate a principled, purposeful and practical relational approach. This results in a Relational Agility that allows them to bridge the generational gaps that exist today between Boomers, Gens (Generation X and Y, broadly), and Millennials; navigate the corporate maze; and collaborate with people to harness their collective talent, thought and effort.

Relational Leaders exercise their Relational Agility by following the Five Principles, but make no mistake: The intention to display Worthy Intent toward others in business and life is the engine that drives the rest. It *must* be present.

Once this principle is established, Relational Leaders consistently deliver on this foundation to inspire performance and contribute to making work and life better.

You will hear a lot more about the Five Principles of the Relational Leader along with case stories and anecdotes about real Relational Leaders from CEOs to driving range owners, all the way to janitors and toll takers who foster these principles throughout their organizations, achieving great business success and the satisfaction that they are making a significant contribution to others.

> The intention to display Worthy Intent toward others in business and life is the engine that drives the rest. It *must* be present.

The Relationship Engine is written to explain each of the Five Principles so that leaders and prospective leaders—from recent grads to seasoned veterans, from Boomers to Gens to Millennials—can see how the conscious, intentional cultivation of effective relationships is foundational to business success. In Part I, I share a simple yet powerful approach that serves as a universal framework for creating relationships that allows for effective collaboration across generations that readers can use immediately.

Part II illustrates and explains that the most effective relationships are the result of paying deliberate, systematic attention to the Five Principles that characterize the behavior of the Relational Leader, and actualizing them in the development of relationships inside and outside complex organizational structures through the Relational Agility Process.

In Part III, I will show that through the clearly defined Relational Agility Process the practical development of these competencies can be a measurable, competitive advantage for Relational Leaders and organizations that understand and practice them.

Finally, throughout this book I have intentionally placed Capability Builders to help you interact with the concepts in order to create actionable ideas that you can try immediately with your important business relationships. And you'll find a glossary at the end to help you keep the new terms straight on your journey through *The Relationship Engine*.

THE FIVE PRINCIPLES OF THE RELATIONAL LEADER

1

THE RELATIONSHIP PARADOX

IF STRONG RELATIONSHIPS ARE critical to leaders and a requirement for their success in an organization, why do so few of them say they actually do anything intentional or systematic toward developing them? Why do I continually hear that "business relationships are difficult"? Sure, it's true that relationships can be difficult, awkward and unpredictable, and they can certainly be challenging to measure. In fact, all of those reasons lead to the opportunity to explore how diversely people view business relationships. In order to do that, please take a few minutes to complete the following sentence:

People like to work with people they . . . _____

You might answer along these lines:

- Like
- Trust
- Know
- Respect
- Are introduced to
- Believe in
- Care about
- Worked with before

- Are challenged by
- View as genuine
- Understand

- Have fun with
- Share common goals with

I call these "relational attributes," attributes we attach to people we like to work with. Hopefully, these are also attributes that others value and see in us. We all instinctively know what goes into a great business relationship and many of these relational attributes relate to our personal relationships as well, and data supports it.

A recent study revealed that 89 percent of senior executives across all major functional areas believe that relationships are the key to their success year over year. Yet, the study went on to indicate that only 24 percent actually do anything *intentionally* about this important element of their success. Remarkably, those 24 percent indicated that they relied on their Customer Relationship Management (CRM) systems to manage their human relationships![1] Good luck with that.

Do you believe that there's really an *R* in CRM systems? I find that human beings put the *R* in CRM systems, so it seems a bit presumptuous to me that these really smart folks are relying on technology to help them accomplish an essential "human calculation." Please think for a minute as to why would they even try to take this shortcut.

The answers are the same.

Business relationships . . .

- Are awkward
- Take an investment of time
- Are challenging to measure
- Cannot be prioritized
- Are unpredictable

Whatever your answer was from the above responses, I assure you someone else has had the same hesitation. Other answers I often hear are "I'm not sure which relationships are the right ones"; "I have over five hundred LinkedIn connections and it's hard to tell where I stand with them"; or "I just don't have relationship building in my DNA." The response I am most surprised by is "I'm not sure of the return on my investment in relationships." This is also amusing because it contradicts what was just declared empirically as the critical factor for success. How many company presidents make the bold statement "My company is built on relationships"? In fact, the study went on to indicate that fewer than 5 percent of organizations actually have any specific strategies for helping their professionals develop and strengthen the relationships required to achieve their goals.

So people do acknowledge the importance of business relationships but since they don't easily fit into a spreadsheet, companies and organizations often ignore or lose their true strategic value and create few systems to directly encourage or support them. Relationships are often left to chance and simply occur in ad hoc patterns in what I call "relational ad-libs." Risky business to say the least when so much is at stake. That's why I call this problem the Relationship Paradox.

THE ESSENCE OF INTENTION: A RESOLVE TO ACT IN A CERTAIN WAY

The real problem starts with the fact that today's companies are so preoccupied with processes and technology, packing more and more complexity into their people's daily work, but with little intentional focus on how to develop the relationships required to drive performance in this environment. We're all attempting to create relationships instinctively and through technology rather than *intentionally*. Even machines need humans!

You can see this problem best in the model that every company uses to codify responsibility—the org chart. So let's start at the beginning to see how companies go wrong.

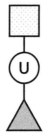

Figure 1-1. This is you.

Figure 1-2. This is you, your boss and your report.

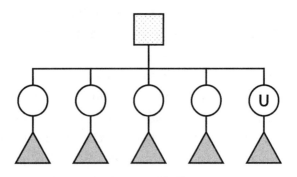

Figure 1-3. This is your department/function.

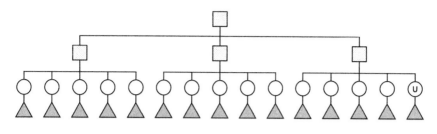

Figure 1-4. This is your division.

Multiply that three, six, maybe a dozen times with more boss layers, plus a board, and you have figure 1-5, your average midsize company:

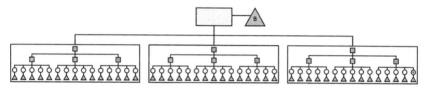

Figure 1-5. This is your midsize company.

The problem is that the charts may show how responsibility flows, but they don't show how actual work flows when humans are involved. That's because you have a relationship with your boss and your report, but to do your job you also have relationships with your colleagues and their reports illustrated by the dotted lines in figure 1-6.

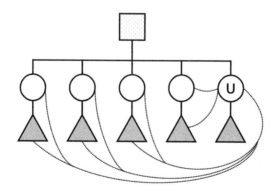

Figure 1-6. These are your department relationships.

And you have relationships in other divisions: Andy in Production, Annie in Finance, Art in Legal, for example.

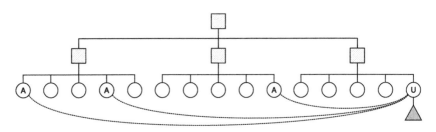

Figure 1-7. These are your division relationships.

Now to pile on even more, think about how the relationship dynamics discussed above are further compounded when we bring people outside of our organizations into our collaborations. Consultants, contractors, partners, government agencies, vendors—they come from different cultures and bring a potentially different set of values and goals, yet are often important to the completion of our projects. For example, strategic alliances usually are accomplished through forming teams from each organization involved, working together to find synergies and incremental added value as a first step toward combining resources and efforts in a more substantive, strategic way.

THE RISE OF AT-WILL RELATIONSHIPS

The above complexity is further exacerbated by what I call At-Will relationships. At-Will relationships are discretionary relationships that are needed to accomplish a business objective. You may have heard the term "at-will employer" or "at-will state," which relates to state employment laws where an employee is more or less hired and employed at the discretion of the employer. When I reflected on this idea in the context of the Relationship Paradox, it struck me that in business today, leaders working on cross-functional teams need help from people around their companies who are more or less At-Will from a relationship standpoint. Let's call these people subject matter experts—colleagues with a deep knowledge on a particular topic. Concurrently, there is a great chance that the subject matter expert who the leader needs to connect with has no knowledge of the need let alone has that need been factored into subject matter expert's performance goals and time commitments. So now you have a leader or a team heading off into the enterprise to accomplish an objective without any real strategy for navigating the discretionary relationships needed to accomplish it. Extend that to relationships that I highlighted outside the company and even more At-Will relationships are needed to accomplish goals and join in all of the fun.

> At-Will relationships are discretionary relationships that are needed to accomplish objectives.

The ability to create and advance these At-Will relationships is the real key to success in the complex organization structures that I shared.

CAPABILITY BUILDER

Reflect on an At-Will relationship that allowed you to move forward with a project or goal.

_____

What stands out that allowed you to connect with that subject matter expert?

_____

ENTERPRISE RELATIONSHIPS

All of this complexity causes the leader to have to extend their influence and create Enterprise Relationships. When we look at Enterprise Relationships the latest research indicates that for large companies, "Entire functions seem to have widely differing relationship values and expectations," as shown in figures 1-8 and 1-9.

Functional Group Research

Please indicate how significant an impact each relationship type has had on your personal and professional success.

Percent Saying "Very Significant Impact"

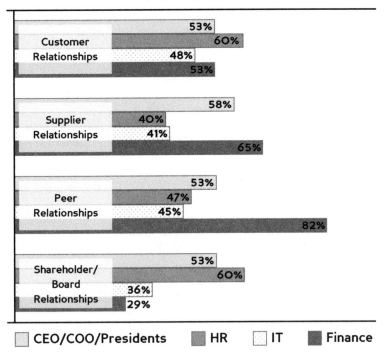

Figure 1-8. Relationship impact on personal success.

Please indicate how significant an impact each relationship type has had on your company's or organization's success.[2]

Percent Saying "Very Significant Impact"

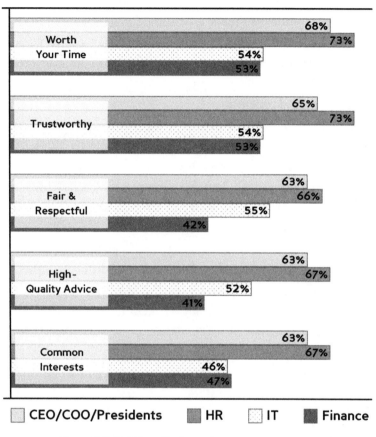

Figure 1-9. Relationship impact on company success.

This makes sense because in general people will follow their leader and if that person values hard skills more than relationships, then that is how people will be hired and integrated into that function's culture and way of working. However, when one of those professionals is added to a team where some members value relationships, things bog down.

Remember, the great promise of technology is that it would enable better cross-functional collaboration in companies, but it turns out that large matrix organizations don't often function very well. Per the research, having different functional leaders, priorities and accountabilities can make cross-functional collaboration challenging and complex. In addition, difference in generation, personality and character among employees can also compound matters. This leads to murky decision-making and significant risk on returns of time and resources.

The equalizing factor across all these complexity variables is productive relationships. Trusting business relationships from functional leader to functional leader and across their teams can usually mitigate and overcome these complexities. A lack of strong and trusting relationships within and across functions limits effective collaborations.

While the previous analysis and figures depict complex human interaction processes, the dynamic leads to additional confirmation of the Relationship Paradox—*company processes are designed and implemented without formal consideration for the strength of employee relationships and their impact on performance. The research indicates that relationships are the key to success!* Reflect for a moment through your real experiences or as an observer on the way that companies spend millions of dollars on important strategic and operational plans—the architecture of business dreams—including pursuits that must be accomplished in order for the plans to succeed. Industry thought leaders and advisers are consulted to help the companies think outside the box, about launching new products and services, opening new offices, implementing the latest technologies, going green and about the wonderful profits and rewards all of this effort will generate. Paradoxically, after investing all of this time and money, they assume or risk that the relationships needed will magically appear and operate effectively. This perceived mysticism is further perpetuated by the ability of a small set of relational "rock stars" who somehow always make things happen and for whom things magically always seem to work out. These rock stars use a series of successive relational ad-libs born of instincts and, in many cases, luck to make the magic happen.

Well, even the best illusionists invest a great deal of planning and practice before they perform their feats. They practice and plan over and over in order to deliver on their mission of creating an outstanding experience for their audience. Similarly, athletes practice every day. LeBron James is one of the top professional basketball players in history, yet every season it seems that he has added something new to his game. One year it was more accurate three-point shooting and the next it was using his left hand closer to the basket. The results speak for themselves. So why then do business professionals stop "practicing"?

RELATIONAL SUPERIORITY COMPLEX

Why do companies and leaders take so much risk when they throw everyone into the corporate soup without any intentions or design consideration for the key relationships that need to develop in order for that team or class of leaders to succeed? In order to understand this miscalculation on the part of companies and leaders, I looked to information we've analyzed over the past ten years. Using a tool called the RQ Assessment to study over twenty-five thousand business relationships across many different industries along with industry research, I learned the following:

- Seventy-eight percent of professionals overestimate the strength of their business relationships.
- Most professionals take relationships for granted.
- Relational intelligence scores remain at average levels year over year.

- Awareness of the strength or the lack thereof increases significantly with Intentionality.
- The best relationships are working at only 45 percent of their potential.[3]

In essence, there exists a "relational superiority complex" where we believe relationships are better than they are and we often do not find out the reality until it is too late. Also Relationship Intentionality is not considered to any great extent during the process design, thereby putting pressure on the company's "people functions" (human resources and organizational dynamics) to interpret competency needs while the process is already rolling along. The tendency is to rely on standard HR professional development programs that develop people skills versus applying actionable relationship strategies into the business process planning. Then, only after the project crashes do we learn that we did not help the people who were put on the project bus through the alignment of actual relationships that were needed for success.

Using a tool like the RQ Assessment, you will notice that relationship strength actually can be measured just like any other attribute that a company is looking to gain insights into. So if we refer to the old management line that "you can only manage what you can measure," and we can in fact measure and observe relationship strength, why then do leaders avoid this incredibly important competency?

PEOPLE ARE DIFFERENT TOO

With our relationship complexity models and research that suggests relationships are operating at less than an optimal level of potential, now let's take a look at the different types of people who work within all of this complexity. Lynn DiBonaventura is an organizational dynamics expert who truly has an insightful view on the pressing need to factor generational differences of people into strategic and operational planning. Lynn summarized the organizational dynamics that I shared earlier as follows:

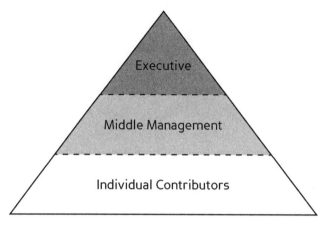

Figure 1-10. Organization 1.0.

Then she went on to explain that Organization 1.0 (figure 1-10) has been the de facto model since the industrial revolution. However, if we factor in the different generations and the way they behave today—Baby Boomers, Gens and Millennials—it adds even more complexity and challenges to the model.

Since the Boomers are generally more comfortable working within the traditional hierarchy, I assigned a triangle to them. The Gens broke into their careers during the cross-functional collaboration movement, so I used wavy parallel lines. And for the Millennials, it may seem like a joke, but you can just put a hashtag (#) down anywhere because they work and think without boundaries, which I believe is a great thing for today's fast-paced, technological environment.

△ Boomers   ≈ Gens   # Millennials

We now have Organization 2.0 where these generations (symbols) are integrated into the model in figure 1-11:

Figure 1-11. Organization 2.0.

Lynn suggested that within the model the generations are interconnected going in all directions laterally and vertically, which is where all of the relationships exist within the company—among employees and between employees, managers and executives. She referred to these connections as "synapses," like the junction between nerve cells in the brain. She said that when human connections are made and relationships happen, it's like powerful synapses firing and this is when work actually gets done in the company. Information gets exchanged, wisdom gets transferred, someone gets mentored or assisted, impactful collaborations take place and an idea gets advanced. "Stuff gets done," in her words.

Then Lynn's summary really surprised me, because she said that when looking at the Organization 2.0 diagram, a lot of us would think of the hierarchical business structure as the *foreground* of the model—the most important overriding structure of the company—because we're accustomed to thinking this way about management, processes and policies. But to her, the real foreground, the most critical aspect of the picture, is the human relationships represented by the interconnections of the generations in the model, since *without these nothing else can happen!*

This interview and subsequent research to this point with Lynn enhanced my theory on relationship complexity and the need for Intentionality when it comes to Relational Leadership and the new value proposition for leaders.

LEADER: THE POWER TO LEAD OTHER PEOPLE

While it's always important to remember this traditional definition of what a leader is and does, it's clear after working with Relational Leaders like Tom Feeney that leadership must adapt to the more complex, cross-functional At-Will relationship scenarios explained above. Leaders have less power to lead other people. The leader's power is challenged by the flattening structures and transparency created by technology and can actually work against them. They can no longer just try to inspire and make sure everyone keeps busy getting things done. In the past, leaders could rely on hierarchy as leverage to get stuff done. However, with the advent of technology, communications and the range of people from Boomers to Millennials who work in companies today, leaders need to focus more on collaboration versus command and control since the power of access to information and pace of action has shifted from the leader to the group. They need to become Relational Leaders by intentionally creating relationships in order to thrive and accomplish their own objectives. As I shared in the introduction, the value proposition for leaders has changed from their ability to command and control to creating an experience for others. Taking the statement that I opened this book with, it now reads: Relational Leaders' success comes through the experience they create for others!

Therefore, as you learn about the Five Principles of the Relational Leader and reflect on how they manifest in your own relationships,

I ask you to think about the following three beliefs in order to overcome the Relationship Paradox and create competitor-proof relationships:

1. Your success involves compelling daily interactions with people.
2. The strength of your relationships is not accidental.
3. Everybody is really smart today so relationship advancement is your last competitive distinguisher.

These beliefs will help make becoming a Relational Leader clearer and actionable for you as you continue your journey through *The Relationship Engine*.

CAPABILITY BUILDER

Think about a time when you had the need to develop an At-Will relationship. Describe how you approached that subject matter expert and what impact it had on your goal:

At-Will relationship:

_____

Check off the At-Will relationship generation:

❑ Boomer   ❑ Gens   ❑ Millennial

Approach:

_____

Result:

_____

The Margin for Error in Business Is Razor-Thin; Why Take Chances on Relationships?

In the world of business, the careful, strategic development of relationships is often the edge needed to increase your chances for success. Whether they're external relationships with customers and business partners or internal relationships when a leader works to build trust and community among her management team, the effective Relational Leader succeeds when she takes a disciplined, structured, intentional approach to this process and recognizes that there is a kind of science to it.

This book is based on both empirical findings and from my experiences with the thousands of Relational Leaders that I have had the opportunity to meet and work with. And after all of those experiences and research, I have landed on the Five Principles that Relational Leaders employ intentionally to break the age-old adage "you either have it or you don't" when it comes to relationships.

This Intentionality runs from the macro planning level all the way to individual daily Relational Micro-moments and manifests in increases of Relational Capital. There's that term again—the value created by people in a business relationship, distinguishing Relational Leaders from their colleagues and competitors.

In the information age, everybody is really smart. So today, relationship advancement is your last competitive distinguisher. Your colleagues and clients might not remember a specific moment when you were able to help your team accomplish a task using your skills alone. But when you approach each interaction with a deliberate intention to positively affect those around you, yes, the results will certainly be reflected numerically. But most importantly, these results manifest themselves in smiles and body language—the way people carry themselves around *you*.

With the margin of error in business so razor-thin, living and applying the Five Principles of the Relational Leaders will transform you into a Relational Leader where even the smallest margins of error will result in your favor.

And in the end, after decades of business evolution, those complex organization charts and relationship models really come down to one simple formula illustrated in figure 1-12:

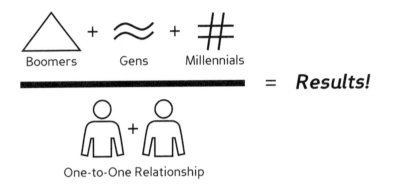

Boomers + Gens + Millennials

One-to-One Relationship

= Results!

Figure 1-12. Generational formula.

This formula certainly does not challenge Einstein's theory of relativity, but in a real way, it is all about relativity. The relationships between diverse human beings are the secret to successful engagement inside and outside of companies and organizations. We have created complex organizational structures that, while well-intended, can create blurred lines rather than sharp connections among people, functions and suppliers.

Leadership and management books are usually about strengthening the solid lines in complex organization charts. However, after all of this research and analysis, I have concluded that sometimes the best approach is not complex, but really simple and straightforward. At the same time, this simplicity can be very profound and in the end looks like Organization 3.0, illustrated in figure 1-13:

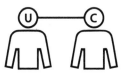

**Figure 1-13. Organization 3.0:
one-to-one relationships.**

If we continue to pile on to already overly complex and over-loaded hierarchical/matrix/cross-functional organization structures, then productivity will fall, decision making will suffer and frustration will prevail. Organization 3.0 does not seek to marginalize or erase all of the thoughtful strategic rationale for today's organizational structures; it merely sets out the simple tenet that eventually people need to connect at an individual level to get stuff done. It reminds me of the thinking behind movie productions. There is a great deal of complexity in making a movie, beginning with the script, moving through funding, selecting actors, going through rehearsals, then shooting and editing the movie and ending up with a product that will be "coming to a theater near you." All of this complexity has one overarching goal—connecting personally with each movie-goer during the two hours they spend in the theater. It's that individual connection that manifests in people talking about the movie, and then a snowball effect happens and more and more people attend the movie. These thousands and sometimes millions of personal, one-to-one connections result in great financial performance and notoriety for the movie company.

Similar to movie productions, Organization 3.0 is about getting back to the basics where people connect individually in powerful ways regardless of organization structure. The structure will exist and evolve based on the management theories du jour; however, Relationship Capital transcends structure. It's really a way to look and become intentional *about the connections* that lead to relational organizations and not the structure. Throughout the rest of this book you'll discover ways to strengthen all of your business relationships and connect with the people who power your business—one by one. *Nothing else matters!*

2

PRINCIPLE #1
Display Worthy Intent

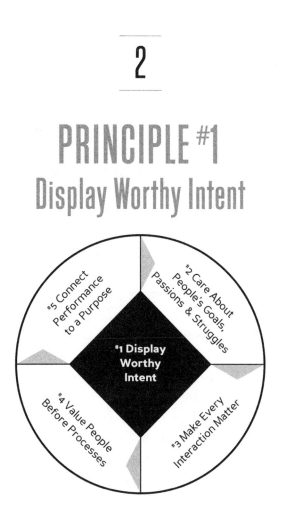

Figure 2-1. Worthy Intent.

HOW DO MOST OF us know intuitively that relationships are the basis of successful businesses and careers? We know this because it's so fundamental that we don't think about it as a competency—we just take it as a given. It's the premise behind professional organizations, conferences, networking events and referrals. It is the reason social media exists and has so wildly revolutionized the worlds of business development, sales, marketing, public relations, project management, career development and talent management—

by creating easy and immediate ways for people to connect with others.

So it is impossible to imagine that managing and leading an organization, a team or a project could be any less dependent on the effective development of relationships. David Armstrong, Ph.D., an expert on leadership, states, "Leadership today is not a trait but a state of relationship between the leader and the other person." Leadership is about understanding how people think and act, what motivates and inspires them, what makes them want to work with you or for you, or advocate for your cause.

Now consider all the concerted, systematic effort that generally goes into any of the following aspects of a business: mergers and acquisitions, new product development, patents, real estate and competitive intelligence, to name a few. Lawyers, accountants, boards of directors, consultants and agencies all get involved, using expert knowledge, market projections, survey data, focus groups and more to ensure that these kinds of decisions get made wisely, precisely and successfully.

But consider the fact that the above initiatives often fail for one simple reason: they do not take adequately into account the *human factor*. Too often, we pay so much attention to the numbers and the data, we forget that it is people, and our relationships with people, that will determine, in the end, whether something succeeds or not. It is people who comprise the working center of Organization 3.0 companies or in Lynn DiBonaventura's words the "foreground" of any organization. Only through relationships can we recruit, hire and retain good people, build enthusiasm around a product, service or project, or get a creative team to come up with great ideas and innovations.

So is it worth our time and effort to examine what, exactly, characterizes the best working relationships? Or to put it my way, what principles or ways make a great Relational Leader tick, and what proven practices, behaviors and qualities can we observe in such leaders that we can learn from? This chapter is all about the foundational principle—the engine that drives everything—that you can observe in great Relational Leaders and the way they act from this basis that I call Worthy Intent.

Trust Is the Inevitable Consequence of Worthy Intent

As I developed this thought, I was concerned that the thought leaders on trust, many of whom are my friends, would challenge me or even take offense, saying, "How dare you elevate an idea ahead of trust and then have the nerve to go on to describe trust as an inevitable consequence?" I can assure them and you that my intentions are *truly worthy* when I declare this because Worthy Intent is so powerful a principle that trust actually must result as a by-product when we exhibit it.

> Worthy Intent *is the inherent promise you make to put the other person's best interest at the core of your business relationship.*

My official definition of Worthy Intent is *the inherent promise you make to put the other person's best interest at the core of your business relationship.*

This concept drives strong relationships—which are essential to powering everything else in business. In order for a person to be willing to trust you, work with you, work for you, collaborate, advocate for your ideas, share innovations and so forth, that person needs to believe that you honestly care about other people's well-being and success, that you have their best interests in mind.

WARMTH AND COMPETENCE

As you can attest from your own experience, we are willing to invest in a relationship when we are confident that the other person not only means us no harm but wishes to actively do good for us and has no hidden agenda. According to Chris Malone, managing partner of Fidelum Partners and coauthor with Susan T. Fiske from Princeton University of the groundbreaking book *The Human Brand*, "intent" is the underlying psychology and dominant factor that drives our behavior.

The whole Warmth and Competence model is about intent (or warmth) and abilities (or competence). Malone explains that we have been hardwired by evolution to try to determine other people's intentions toward us based on body language, facial expressions, tone of voice and so on. Back when we were primitive, correctly judging someone's intentions meant life or death and was more predictive of your survival than judging someone's competence or ability. This core instinct is still baked into us and it has not changed in thousands of years. These conclusions have been validated over the past twenty years across forty countries with Dr. Fiske as the leading authority on this concept.

As it turns out, there is extensive academic research that helps explain why the principle of Worthy Intent is so powerful in influencing others. For our ancestors who lived thousands of years ago, the ability to recognize people, to correctly judge their intentions and to build trusting relationships was crucial to their survival. Today, hardwired by evolution, we instinctively judge others when we interact with them, assessing them along the same two key social dimensions that our ancestors did: warmth and competence (figure 2-2).

First, we assess the person's warmth toward us. Are you a friend or foe? Will you help or hurt me? Will you give to me or take from me? Warmth is judged by assessing whether one is kind, friendly and good-natured; whether one appears sincere, honest, moral and trustworthy; and whether one possesses an accommodating orientation and is perceived as helpful, tolerant, fair, generous and understanding.

Second, we assess the person's overall level of competence to understand how successful they would be in carrying out their intentions toward us. Are you stronger or weaker than I am? How much power do you possess? What special resources do you have that make you capable of helping or hurting me? Competence is judged by assessing whether you possess special resources, skills, creativity or intelligence that grants you an advantage. Do you appear efficient, capable, skillful, clever and knowledgeable? Do you seem to possess the confidence and ability to carry out your plans?

Warmth Assessment		Competence Assessment		Emotional Response		Behavioral Response
Warm	+	Competent	->	Admiration	->	Attraction
				Pride		Affiliation
						Alliance
Cold	+	Competent	->	Envy	->	Begrudging Cooperation
						Obligatory Association
Warm	+	Incompetent	->	Sympathy	->	Indifferent Neglect
				Pity		
Cold	+	Incompetent	->	Contempt	->	Rejection
				Disgust		Disassociation

Figure 2-2. Warmth and Competence assessment.

The answers to these questions guide our mental, emotional and behavioral responses toward people, affecting what we think of them, how we feel toward them and what we do to embrace or avoid them.

We retreat from or defend ourselves against threatening people who are capable of hurting us, while we safely ignore those who mean us harm but who are less capable. We form alliances with those with good intentions who bring competence and skill to our relationship.

Further, warmth judgments always occur first and carry greater weight than competence judgments. We are particularly sensitive to changes in warmth and actively search for behaviors that disconfirm that someone has warm intentions toward us. Competence judgments are more forgiving; someone who has been perceived as competent is allowed a few slips in competence before we adjust our overall assessment.

These Warmth and Competence assessments are remarkably strong predictors of how we feel and act toward others. Social psychologists estimate that these two simple assessments predict more than 80 percent of our overall assessments of people.[1]

Since warmth perceptions are by definition an attempt to discern the intentions of others, when we practice the principle of Worthy Intent, we demonstrate the warmth and goodwill needed for them to trust and become loyal to us. So it's the basic psychology of human trust and loyalty that makes the principle of Worthy Intent so powerful in our relationships with others, both personally and professionally.

If you want to build a "warm" culture and experience for your colleagues, it has to start with every interaction the people in the company have with each other and those they work with in business. And it is does not have to be complicated by any means, based on the following examples:

Warm Behaviors
- I made a mistake and I am going to take care of it for you.
- I cannot help you but I know someone who can.
- I say I'll call you back and I do.
- I put a smiley face next to your name on your order.

Malone concludes, "The little inexpensive things that are 'warmth' related have a much greater impact than expensive 'competence' related things. Therefore, the more of the little things you cover the better the chances you have to create trust and loyalty."

From my perspective, warmth is the underpinning of Worthy Intent. Malone cites that every year there seems to be some new theory of how the business and leadership world works. He asked me, "How can all of these leadership ideas and theories all be true? What is the common thread?" He believes that *Worthy Intent is the underlying psychology that allows all of the models to work.*

Therefore, once this foundation of Worthy Intent is established, there is almost no limit to what can be accomplished through a business or personal relationship. The people at the Children's Hospital of Philadelphia knew this when they went out of their way to track my son Brett and me down as we rushed there to be with Grant who was injured and likely very scared. After this experience, we felt so convinced of their Worthy Intent and their genuine concern for our family's well-being that there is no other hospital we would choose in the event of another need for one of our family members' children. This results in even more opportunities for them to treat children and while this is the noblest of their pursuits, it also adds a great deal to the health system's bottom line. Unsurprisingly, the Children's Hospital of Philadelphia consistently ranks as one of the top pediatric centers in the United States.

CAPABILITY BUILDER

Have you ever engaged with any of the following?

1. A barista at Starbucks

2. A canvasser in the mall

3. A retail salesperson on the appliance sales floor

4. Kids fund-raising outside a supermarket

My guess is that everyone has had one if not all of these experiences and various perspectives and feelings about how they went. Let's look at the one that may be the most challenging for many of us to deal with—retail salesperson. Many times our first response is to walk away or even shun their approach by curtly suggesting that you will contact them when you are ready. But if we go back to the Warmth and Competence theory, we find that if that person somehow was able to demonstrate warmth in their approach, then we likely did not completely shun their outreach. For example, if the salesperson said, "We have a lot of great stuff on sale that I would be happy to help you with" (competence), we'd probably respond, "I am just browsing." But if he started with, "Hi, welcome to Acme Appliance. My name is Jim. Feel free to take all the time you need and I will be available should you have any questions" (warmth). There is a good chance we will feel more warmth about Jim and thus the relationship has more of a chance to evolve.

Please recall a time when you responded positively to one of the four approaches mentioned above, whether it was warmth or competence based, and how did your interaction conclude?

Approach:

_____

Warmth or competence initially demonstrated:

_____

Result:

_____

PRINCIPLE #1

PRACTICE WITH A PURPOSE

Mike is not a CEO in the general sense of the word. He owns a small business, a golf driving range, but it's not your typical golfing range because Mike is also the ideal Relational Leader who has created a true destination for the members of our community.

I met him several years ago while struggling with my swing in one of his tee boxes.

"What club are you hitting?" he asked.

"My 4-iron," I replied.

"How often do you use it?"

"Not much. Maybe three times a round," I said.

"How many swings have you taken with it today?"

"Most of this bucket."

"What's your best club?"

"My 6."

"Would you mind taking a few swings with it?" he asked.

So I hit several balls with my 6-iron. The results were much better.

That's when he finally introduced himself, extended his hand and said, "Hi, I'm Mike."

I still wasn't sure what he did, though. While he wore a golf shirt, his demeanor was more like that of a person doing manual work rather than giving golf lessons. He suggested that since I am doing so well with the 6-iron that I consider choking up a bit on my 4-iron, almost making it into a 6-iron in length.

During my next trip to the range, I brought my son Brett along. Brett was five years old at the time, and as with some five-year-olds, he was not sitting still for very long. As he ventured from tee box to tee box, he eventually ran into Mike. Mike immediately engaged Brett by asking him if he wanted to help him pick up the empty buckets and then they can "make a very tall mountain of buckets." Of course Brett jumped at the opportunity.

In the meantime, guess who had more focused time to work on his game? Me!

Mike eventually stopped over and asked how I am hitting with my 4-iron. He remembered! I mentioned that it's improving and demonstrated a few shots. Although my shots were not going as far as they should with a 4-iron, they were very accurate and as I kept swinging it struck me how comfortable I was hitting in front of Mike. This was not the case in the past as I was always very conscious with other instructors of how good (actually poor) my golf swing was. He suggested one grip adjustment and then went on his rounds picking up the empty golf buckets with Brett, while commenting to numerous customers and his employees:

"Mornin', Sarah, how was your round yesterday?"

"Sam, great job mowing the putting green! You better head home so you can make football practice on time!"

"Tina, congratulations on getting the new teaching position."

And on and on, as he moved up through the hitting tees.

Eventually, Brett was invited to ride around in the Ranger cart that picks up the golf balls.

After a few more trips to the range, I finally figured out that Mike actually owned the place. During that time, I observed him being completely immersed with each of his customers and employees and not once did I ever see him trying to sell an actual paid golf lesson or dictating work to his staff. Everything was about the experience he created for other people. *In other words, their goals were first in line.*

When it comes to this powerful principle of Worthy Intent that I first consciously discovered through the children's hospital experience with Grant, Mike is one of the first Relational Leaders who comes to my mind. From a competence standpoint, Mike is a five-time winner of the Philadelphia Amateur Open and was a PGA pro as well. However, with all of his competence in playing golf, he could not find the time for his real passion: helping people actually play golf. One day, I asked Mike about his grand plan to create his driving range. He shared that the owner of the property "really liked me and my idea" about creating a golf experience that anyone could enjoy and not be encumbered by finances or a lack of prestige. He explained to the owner, "Golf is difficult enough. Why should people have to be self-conscious or inhibited on top of it?" A Worthy Intent, indeed. Hmmm, remember that people like to work with people they *like*? And that leading with warmth is the best approach when launching a new business relationship?

Today, the sign on Mike's "learning facility," as he calls it, states: "Practice with a Purpose." Whenever I see this sign, I relate it to being intentional about relationships! Think about it. If you are going to try to get better at golf, then you need to have a purposeful or practical way about you. You can swing a thousand times, but if you are not gripping the club correctly or not picking out a target your results will be random at best. The same goes for business relationships.

Mike's customers all started going to his range with one common goal—to get better at the crazy game of golf. If you stop by Mike's golf range today, you will find children taking clinics while their moms and dads hang out on the deck that Mike built with his own hands to make his customers more comfortable. Golfers like me hitting balls in a very relaxed, collegial environment. Players from just about every ethnic and economic background are socializing in between swings. Most importantly, we all trusted Mike with our common goals for golf and even our kids due to his Worthy Intent toward us not just as golfers and customers but as people.

CAPABILITY BUILDER

Think back to the Organization 3.0 model of One-to-One Relationships from chapter 1 and describe how attributes of Mike's golf learning facility reflect that model:

_____

_____

Mike has created a destination in our community—a place to just hang around, hone our games and catch up with friends. Mike loves to share the following: "People come here and hang out all day and sometimes they never even pick up a club!"

Now it's your turn. Think about and write down the top three attributes that describe the experience you create for your colleagues when you are working together:

1. _____

2. _____

3. _____

DISPLAYING WORTHY INTENT

As I begin sharing more thoughts and experiences in relation to the foundational principle of Worthy Intent—the inherent promise you make to put the other person's best interests at the core of your business relationship—I want to be careful to state my belief that most humans *do* have the other person's best interest at heart. I am not making a judgment of any kind to the contrary. Therefore, the ability to display Worthy Intent is grounded in the belief that you are going in by putting the other person's goals or needs ahead of your own.

Displaying Worthy Intent is both a perpetual state of being and an intention, a resolve to act. This principle needs to *be* and exist within us before the other principles can be applied. And most importantly, if you think about it, how can trust emerge and be sustained in a business relationship without Worthy Intent?

However, it all comes down to your Worthy Intent actually being *displayed and validated by the behaviors you experience coming back to you.* For example, if I were to ask you to take a minute to write down why people love to work with you, my guess is that you would respond, "I keep my commitments," "I always follow up," "I'm responsive" and so on. Next reflect on how you validate that you have actually fostered these intentions with your colleague, which is the real key to Worthy Intent. So to explore how this applies to you further, please take a minute and complete the following Capability Builder regarding how Worthy Intent manifests when people work with you.

CAPABILITY BUILDER

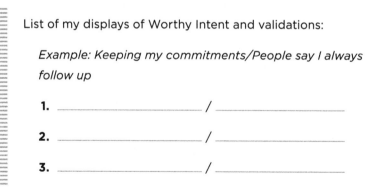

List of my displays of Worthy Intent and validations:

Example: Keeping my commitments/People say I always follow up

1. _____ / _____

2. _____ / _____

3. _____ / _____

Therefore, to display Worthy Intent is not just about having the other person's best interest at heart, but also about their acknowledgment of your Worthy Intent based on the demonstrated behaviors that result when you are interacting. Think about someone who you believe has Worthy Intent toward you at work. My guess is that this person's intentions could be validated by some of the following behaviors:

- Always in the moment
- Transparency
- Loyalty
- Has fun
- Keeps confidences

So How Can You Display Worthy Intent?

There are two drivers for understanding and ultimately allowing us to display Worthy Intent:

1. The thoughtfulness to put others' goals ahead of your own
2. The ability to assess the behaviors of the other person

▶ Driver #1:
The thoughtfulness to put others' goals ahead of your own

Now let's start exploring the first driver to display Worthy Intent by connecting it to the activity that I asked you to consider during the introduction when I asked you to complete the statement:

People like to work with people they . . .

I shared that I typically hear like, know, trust, respect and so on. However, when I inquire further and ask my participants to think about their very best business relationship and to get that person's face in their mind's eye, you'll note that I included the following in the group of responses:

People like to work with people they SHARE COMMON GOALS WITH!

In my firm's work with companies and organizations around the world, we have learned that business relationships are operating at the highest level when both colleagues share common goals. This takes us to the first key capability required to be able to display

Worthy Intent—the thoughtfulness to put the other person's goals ahead of their own. Let's go back to Mike and his amazing driving range. Take a look at how Mike observes and displays Worthy Intent (figure 2-3):

Mike's Observations/ Remembering	Mike's Displayed Worthy Intentions
Ed's poor swing	Suggesting easy ways to build confidence
Brett creating stir	Creating a fun project to occupy his time
Sarah's round of golf the previous day	Sincerely inquiring about her round
Sam's three-putting	Concern over his friend's performance
Tina's new teaching position	Discussing something important to her outside of golf

Figure 2-3. Mike's Worthy Intent.

▶ *Driver #2:*
The ability to assess the behaviors of the other person

The second key driver for understanding the existence of Worthy Intent in the business relationship is to assess the behaviors of the person you are working with to validate whether they truly believe you have their best interests at heart. There are times when we hear the word "behavior" that we tend to think a degree in psychology or sociology is required to even hold a conversation about it. Well, this should not limit our ability to observe human behavior; in fact, it may make it even easier if we don't think too deeply about the behaviors we see coming back to us in business relationships.

I have found through observation and conversations (plus it is easy writing a book when you stay with the same metaphor!) that golf caddies are possibly the greatest non-degreed observers of human behavior. I have learned that a caddie knows whether his player will hit a good shot prior to even gripping the club based on how the player interacts with him during the "golf shot strategy" conversation. When the conversation ends and the player confidently goes through his pre-shot routine, that's a good sign to the caddie that his player is about to hit a scoring shot. However, if the conversation ends and the caddie observes more grass being tossed into the air, gripping, regripping and other pre-shot idiosyncrasies, the caddie is likely to witness a poor result after the golfer eventually swings. The key is that the caddie is simply observing the behavior of the person he is working with in relation to the task at hand, not looking for anything deep or psychological.

For example, in business it's not that difficult to observe that your colleague is focused on your conversation or conversely cuts your meetings short or does not respond to your email requests, among other behaviors.

CAPABILITY BUILDER

Please take a few minutes to complete figure 2-4, a table of behaviors you have observed and experienced when working with colleagues during your career:

Affirming Relational Behaviors	Negative Relational Behaviors

Affirming Relational Behaviors	Negative Relational Behaviors
Responds quickly to correspondence	Ignores your outreach
In the moment during discussions	Multitasking with email during discussions
Shares confidences	Rarely goes off the meeting topic
Makes extra meeting time	Ends meetings earlier than needed
Introduces you to others	Avoids including you in other interactions

Figure 2-4. Affirming and Negative Relational Behaviors

DISPLAYING WORTHY INTENT PAYS OFF

After over twenty years of visiting with Mike at his driving range, aka learning facility, he remains one of my favorite Relational Leaders. He builds trust every day as a consequence of his Worthy Intent toward others—no conditions, no agendas, just continuing to observe his customers' and friends' behavior and aligning his own behavior in a way that always puts them first. By the way, Mike's business continues to thrive in a golf industry that is not growing, by retaining employees both permanent and part-time year after year along with attracting more and more golfers like me. Recently a PGA player who has competed in nine major championships joined Mike at his range. Stu could have worked anywhere, but there is something truly compelling about Mike and the experience he creates for others.

Trust is the inevitable consequence of Worthy Intent.

3

PRINCIPLE #2
Care About People's Goals, Passions and Struggles

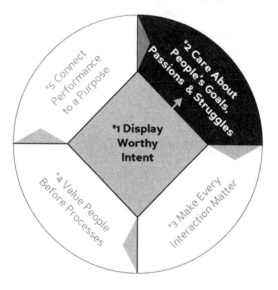

Figure 3-1. Relational Leadership.

YOU MAY HAVE HEARD the following from an old comedy, either as a joke or perhaps in a real conversation:

"Enough about me, tell me about you. What do you think about me?"

Nothing is a bigger turn-off than people who only want to talk about themselves, their goals and their needs. We've all been in business networking events and situations where everyone is in a panic to make their way around the room and introduce themselves to as many people as possible before the guest speaker starts or the food runs out. You exchange a few friendly sentences, and if you're lucky, find a couple of points of common interest, trade business cards and shake hands. You usually leave not knowing much about anyone and not having had a chance to make a genuine connection.

Worse, today we're obsessed with "friending" hundreds of people on Facebook, following each other on Twitter and amassing contacts on LinkedIn. This accumulation of what I call *ethereal* relationships with few concrete ties to business performance too often leads to a lot of nothing but digital activity. Conversely, nothing is more powerful in a business relationship than a company or someone who shows genuine interest in other people, especially in this age of electronic communication and rapidly advancing technology.

Teleflex: Building Relationships Through Progress Conversations

Teleflex is a leading medical device manufacturing company with a global reach that has had a tremendous amount of success focusing on Principle #2: Care About People's Goals, Passions and Struggles. Its core values define for employees the culture they can expect working at the company as reflected by its motto: "People at the center of all we do."

Shortly after Benson Smith became CEO of Teleflex, he held a global conference call with his new professional workforce. He introduced a process that had served him well as a medical device executive: the Work Planning and Review System (WPRS). At its base level, WPRS is a "progress conversation" that takes place on a regular basis between managers and employees. In the previous chapter, Chris Malone suggested that it was all about the warm "little things" versus the expensive competent things that made the difference at the brand and individual level in organizations.

WPRS is a simple process that has made a major impact. Employees document short-term objectives on a form and send it to their manager. Managers meet with employees to discuss priorities, and they review progress from the previous period. Benson Smith uses WPRS with the top leaders in the company and the practice cascades through the professional workforce. Pretty straightforward, right?

Frequent performance discussions were familiar to the sales force, but it was a new concept for other exempt professionals. Early on, some thought WPRS seemed excessive and micromanaging; they complained about documentation. But using WPRS that first year demonstrated the value of regular progress conversations. And having a form that tracked progress supported more informed merit and bonus compensation decisions.

The process exemplifies several leadership best practices:

- Managers can recognize great work closer to the time it occurred.
- If an employee misses a goal because of competing priorities, managers can remove obstacles so that high-priority projects can get back on track.
- Beyond work activities, WPRS tracks employee development goals and progress.
- Employees can talk about career aspirations.
- Managers can identify experiences and training to support career growth.

And at Teleflex, high-performing managers use the conversations to show interest in employees' lives outside of work too.

Studies indicate that achieving progress and recognition are among the most satisfying aspects of work. WPRS supports that recognition, but it also serves a much higher cause than a progress report. The conversations that take place over time are building trust that someone cares about your work and is there to support you. And managers are becoming stronger coaches and mentors.

Having a CEO that speaks about and practices these leadership concepts has helped make Teleflex a relationship-centric, performance-focused organization and a great place to work. From an engagement standpoint, one of the highest-rated responses to employee surveys at Teleflex is: "I know what is expected of me at work."

Cam Hicks, vice president of global human resources and employee communications at Teleflex, says, "The WPRS has been a powerful tool for us to build engagement across our organization. By ensuring that every manager has a regular, dedicated and focused one-on-one interaction with each of their direct reports, it has been a concrete way for us to entrench one of our core values: putting people at the center. It's one of those regular conversations that helps to build understanding and clarity in the most important relationship that exists in the workplace: between an individual and their immediate manager."

UNIVERSAL FRAMEWORK FOR RELATIONSHIPS

I really like sharing the Teleflex "progress conversations" process with emerging Relational Leaders because after establishing an understanding of the foundational and unavoidable principle of Worthy Intent, Teleflex's process is an intentional, straightforward example of Principle #2: Care About People's Goals, Passions and Struggles. By way of translation, people have business and personal goals; passions or causes, the things they care deeply about; and ultimately, struggles just like every human being experiences. The WPRS approach creates intentional opportunities for conversations that lift up and allow for engagement around the Relational GPS (Goals, Passions and Struggles) of fellow Teleflex employees. As simple as this sounds, I find the approach profound because with work so frantic today, we may tend to forget the key concept that I mentioned earlier: "Success comes through the experience we create for others!" That experience, aka engagement, begins with our ability to learn about and align with our colleagues' Relational GPS. Just like our car's GPS is the road map to our travel success, Relational GPS is the road map to unlocking the potential to create, advance and sustain our business relationships.

In fact, if we think about the three generations that I divided all of us into during chapter 1—Boomers, Gens and Millennials— applying or caring about Relational GPS is really a universal way to connect with each group by getting to the GPS of the person we are working with, regardless of generation. Relational GPS spans the generations and bridges the gaps that exist because

> Relational GPS is about really knowing people, not just knowing about them.

it is specific to the person we are engaged with, not their generation. I've known some "old souls" who are Millennials as well as some Boomers who think more like Millennials. The ease of applicability of this concept really surprises me because with something that is as complex as cross-generational relationships, you would expect an equally challenging approach would be required. However, if we think back to Organization 3.0, it all comes down to connecting with the other human being and meeting them where they are through their Relational GPS.

CAPABILITY BUILDER

So let's continue on with Principle #2 and challenge ourselves by answering the following:

When do business relationships really begin?

_____

_____

My customers and colleagues often look at me in confusion when I ask them this. Their responses include: "when I take them to lunch," "when we meet for the first time," "when they join the project team" or "with our first conversation." All of these are valid answers; however, Relational Leaders are seeking a much deeper connection to the human being they are interacting with for the first time.

Therefore, I believe and even declare that business relationships really begin when one party or the other starts sharing what matters most to them—a goal, a passion or a struggle. Principle #2: Care About People's Goals, Passions and Struggles is all about the universal framework and concepts that you can take from this book and use for the rest of your business and personal lives. Most everything that a colleague or customer shares with us can fall into one of these three categories. In fact, if you take only one thing from this book (beyond the value of when we display Worthy Intent, which is a must!), the concept of Relational GPS would be my suggestion.

So if we take a closer look at Relational GPS, it's an example of what marketing experts call a "discontinuous innovation." A discontinuous innovation is a marketing term for something that completely obliterates or makes obsolete whatever preceded it. For example, when was the last time you listened to music on cassette? Just as the cassette made the eight-track obsolete, the CD came along and made the cassette obsolete, then the mp3 has made the CD obsolete—and now music streaming services are beginning to make the mp3 obsolete.

Global positioning systems (GPS) in our cars and phones are another example of a discontinuous innovation that has become a way of life for us as we travel, taking much of the guesswork out of following directions—something our parents' generation struggled with even with paper maps on the dashboard. It amazes me how accurate these GPS directions are even in construction zones. As I mentioned previously, they are the new road map to our travel success.

Correspondingly, a major capability of the Relational Leader's road map to success in developing exceptional experiences is to understand the mechanics of the Relational GPS for each colleague. I include Relational GPS in the list of discontinuous innovations because I continue to hear, "How do I capture or keep track of all of the information that my colleagues share with me?" For customers, we attempt to keep detailed accounts in CRM systems, which include everything about the business contact. Then whenever someone needs to learn about a customer, we simply look up her profile in the system.

But how can that apply to all of our colleague and team member relationships? How can we use it for cross-generational differences and to overcome challenges? Sure, we may be prompted through LinkedIn regarding something about their birthday or work anniversary coming up or write down an aspect we learn about their family. But I had not found any consistent, simple approach to tracking all of this important information—especially business goals and struggles—outside of CRM systems. Plus, there is just not enough time to keep track of so many potential details in any formal way.

Relational GPS: Relationship Shorthand

This opportunity spurred me to develop a shorthand road map for Relational Leaders so they can be as intentional about their relationships as they are about the project they are working on (see figure 3-2). As I mentioned earlier, the most important information that is shared between individuals can be summarized into three categories—goals, passions and struggles. Relational GPS is all about identifying your colleague's business and personal goals, causes or passions (things they care deeply about), and struggles, which every human being has.

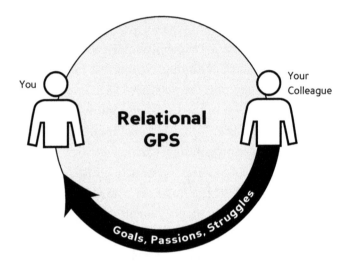

Figure 3-2. Relational GPS.

Here's an example of capturing Relational GPS:

- Important Business Relationship: Jeff
    - Goals: Attempting to acquire new business prior to retiring
    - Passions: Working with nonprofits to help advance their causes
    - Struggles: Seeking a competent successor

Depending on how well you know a person, you may be able to fill in all three or just one goal, passion or struggle. The challenge is not what you know today, but what you can learn firsthand over time.

CAPABILITY BUILDER

Please write down the name of a key relationship you need to launch or advance in order to achieve your goals this year. Then fill in what you really know in relation to their Relational GPS. Can you do this for your top five, ten or fifteen business relationships?

Important Relationship	Goals	Passions	Struggles

I find that many of my clients think they really know their own colleagues and customers until they consider the relationships using the Relational GPS shorthand. Most are surprised at how little they know but how easy it is to learn about Relational GPS. It is simply a matter of being intentional about that person and what they care about. However, not having this info puts you at a disadvantage relationally and ultimately adds risk to any project or process you are developing. As I shared earlier, people want to work with people they believe in before they will share or work with them on common goals.

The challenge with learning about Relational GPS, as with putting the other person first in Principle #1: Display Worthy Intent, is helping leaders understand that it is really about the *other person's* GPS and not their own. Trying to launch the relationship without determining the other people's GPS is like driving cross-country without a map, because unless they've shared aspects of their goals, passions and struggles with you, the relationship not only hasn't really begun, but it also has no direction. So how does it all start?

With Credibility.

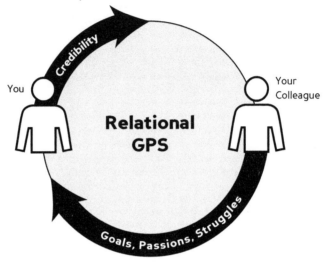

Figure 3-3. Credibility.

Few things are as impactful and powerful as Credibility when it comes to a business relationship and learning about Relational GPS. Credibility is defined as "the power to elicit belief." Unless someone truly *believes* that you have the ability to help them solve their problem, why would they want to work with you? Conversely, if they cannot truly believe that you are credible with your own goals, why would they commit their valuable time to help you? Why would they even move another step and give you the opportunity to work together in the context of the business relationship? Therefore, once your colleague truly *believes* that you can help her deal with her goals, passions and struggles or vice versa to some degree on both a professional and a personal level, you can advance through the work process much more meaningfully and successfully.

The challenge, of course, is that colleagues—who are people, after all—are generally not inclined to share their goals, passions and struggles with anyone they do not deem as credible or competent. Yet, until colleagues begin to share these with you, the business relationship is parked in neutral.

So to get the relationship out of neutral and moving, we must build our ability to listen, to remember, to ask great questions, to share relevant information and in essence to really care and be thoughtful about the answers we hear. Again in Chris Malone's words, "We need to demonstrate 'warmth.'"

CAPABILITY BUILDER

Practice Listening

Get together with a friend or colleague over a coffee break or lunch and explain that you are working on your listening skills. Ask him to share something with you that you may not know about one of his goals, passions or struggles. Let's say they share a goal, then you inquire about that goal for four to five minutes *without* talking about yourself—whether you have a similar goal, how you accomplished it and so on. During this time, do the following:

1. Work on validating what you have heard.

2. Resist the urge to offer solutions, interpret or judge.

3. Continue to ask for more information.

4. Debrief with the person after you are finished about what they experienced and how you conducted your inquiry.

You will find that, although the time allotment may have seemed like a long time initially, it will go by very quickly and you will likely go past that time without even realizing it. While this is an exercise and in "real-life" business scenarios you will likely need to interject a few things to validate or acknowledge the information you are receiving, the approach hones your ability to:

- Really listen intently and care about the answers
- Become believable (credible) to your colleague through your inquiries
- Be better equipped to take the relationship to the next level

After your colleague begins believing that you have Worthy Intent toward him and the knowledge and capability to work through the challenge, he will share more and more of his Relational GPS, and the relationship will begin to flourish.

Remember, a new colleague or business contact doesn't care about your ideas or solutions yet. Right now, this person is still determining whether he likes you and believes what you say—in other words, finds you credible. Your idea or recommendation has no relevance at this point in the relationship. The other person is testing your degree of warmth!

The questions *the other person* has at this point are:

- Do I like you?
- Can I trust you with my team?
- Will you embarrass me?
- Will you come through in the clutch?
- Why are you wearing such an awful tie?

In many cases, those initial assessments are more emotional than rational, but as with the theory of Warmth and Competence, most people are seeking warm intentions before they care about how smart you are. Therefore, until we are deemed credible by our colleague, the relationship is still one-way versus mutual. So here are some of my favorite "Credibility indicators" that Relational Leaders observe in their own business relationships:

Credibility Indicators

- Willing to have an extended conversation beyond the time scheduled
- Responds quickly to correspondence, usually within twenty-four hours
- Changes existing plans to extend meeting time
- Willing to share some initial Relational GPS
- Volunteers personal common ground early in the business relationship

CAPABILITY BUILDER

Think back to a situation where you developed Credibility by asking questions rather than presenting ideas. How did you open the interaction? What was your colleague's reaction? Were you prepared to inquire beyond a surface level on the topic you inquired about?

So now that we have begun applying Relational GPS by becoming credible, we have an opportunity to demonstrate that we really care and are thoughtful about what is being shared by moving to the second quality at play in business relationships: Integrity.

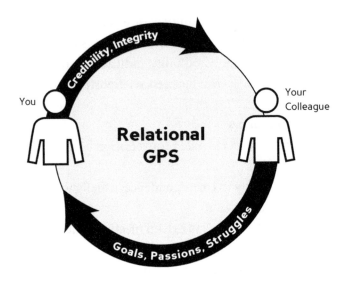

Figure 3-4. Integrity.

At some point, your colleague will begin to share Relational GPS with you, and that indicates you have reached a level of believability to keep advancing into more of a mutual business relationship. You have crossed the Credibility threshold. Be aware that when you can identify a goal, passion or struggle, the relationship is just beginning. Now you have a chance to begin working together, which affords the next opportunity to begin to display Integrity by what I like to call "keeping your promises."

Business professionals will call these commitments, but at a human level, they are promises and the more we keep the better chance we have to advance the relationship and evolve as a Relational Leader. This reminds me of a recent commercial I watched that involved a trucking company. Their tagline in the ad was "Helping you keep your promises." This tagline or sound bite struck me because in the context of delivering boxes and all kinds of freight, the trucker is ultimately delivering on his own customers' promises. Reflecting on this a little deeper reminded me that, ultimately, each delivery is personal to the receiver, just like in Organization 3.0, where

Relational Leaders build relationships one at a time and extend them across their complex organizations. Integrity ties to the principle of Worthy Intent when it allows us to demonstrate honest and truthful motivations for our actions. The trucker's tagline is the first step in connecting Relational GPS with Integrity. This transition, which appears subtle, is huge in the realm of launching and advancing your business relationships because the relationship moves from a one-way to an emerging mutual relationship when our colleague begins to engage us around doing things together.

Here are five ways to build trust:
1. Be open and honest about issues.
2. Share factual information, not hype to advance your ideas.
3. Follow through on commitments.
4. Go ugly early—share bad news as soon as you can.
5. Do business on a handshake whenever possible.

Research by the Great Places to Work Institute indicates that no interaction is trust neutral. Trust will increase or decrease before, during and after your interactions. So now that you have begun to build trust by sharing and following up on commitments together, the relationship is advancing. As with Credibility, here are some "Integrity indicators" that Relational Leaders observe in their own business relationships to ensure that trust is increasing:

Integrity Indicators
- Willing to share business goals and why they are trying to accomplish them
- Willing to share business problems and issues that are holding them back from their goals
- Willing to make and keep commitments
- Willing to share appropriate levels of confidential information

- Willing to include you in their planning processes based on the value you bring to the process

One of my favorite sayings about Integrity is "Secrets draw people together." It's not that business has to be cloak-and-dagger, but think about how powerfully your Credibility and Integrity have evolved with your colleagues when they share confidences with you.

CAPABILITY BUILDER

Recall an interaction where you believe trust increased in your relationship and why. Did your Credibility come into play and what made you credible?

You are now ready to become even more "authentic" with your colleague.

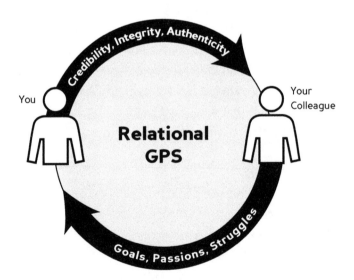

Figure 3-5. Authenticity.

If I were to ask you to define "Authenticity," you might reply:

- Real
- Genuine
- Being yourself
- True to yourself
- You know it when you see it

And so on. I believe that Authenticity is the most difficult quality to demonstrate due to the degree of bravery it requires for us at times to be our unvarnished selves. For example, sometimes we may get caught up in our image and how other leaders or customers may view us if we do not have all the answers. The authentic phrase "I don't know" can be refreshing for colleagues when they work with us and open doors to a productive conversation around this shared struggle. The authentic acknowledgment of not being the smartest person in the room can lead to the opportunity to develop even better solutions.

CAPABILITY BUILDER

Please reflect on Authenticity and write down the names of two authentic people:

1. Someone you know:

_____

2. Someone you know of:

_____

For the first one, you may have listed a relative or someone you know very well or may have worked closely with. For the second one, you may have responded with Warren Buffett, Queen Elizabeth II, Bill Gates, the Pope or various other leaders.

My guess is that for both responses the people you identified seem authentic from a positive standpoint. But consider someone who tends to be less admired, from a personality standpoint. Do you view them as authentic? You may have come up with Steve Jobs or Donald Trump as responses to this prompt. As we explore why I mentioned these names, the concept of Authenticity being the bravest quality will become even clearer. While we may not admire various leaders for their approach or bravado, it is difficult not to admire them for being true to themselves. That's what makes Authenticity so real, and if we are not who we really are, do we actually have Integrity in our business relationships?

While our opinion of the Authenticity of various public figures is just that, our opinion or perception, here is my list of Relational Leader "Authenticity indicators" for people we know and work with:

Authenticity Indicators
- Willing to personally introduce you to other business contacts
- Willing to share their own real experiences
- Willing to be informal when formal behavior is generally expected
- Willing to act as a career-spanning reference, putting their own relationship on the line
- No time seems to have passed when you get together to catch up

CAPABILITY BUILDER

Reflect on a business relationship when you were comfortable being your authentic self at an early stage in the relationship. Record the business relationship below and describe what prompted you to become genuine sooner than you anticipated.

Business relationship:

_____

Why did Authenticity emerge?

_____

My favorite comment about Authenticity remains, "Be yourself, everybody else is taken." It's so much easier just being who we are in every interaction.

Your Credibility, Integrity and Authenticity are the essential qualities that allow Relational Leaders to build the distinctive value of Relational Capital with their colleagues and contacts, as shown in figure 3-6.

Credibility + Integrity + Authenticity = Relational Capital

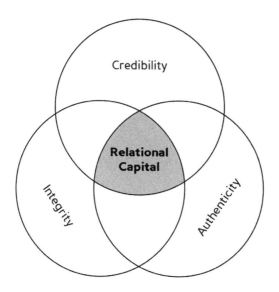

Figure 3-6. The Essential Qualities of Relational Capital.

We all have these qualities; the key point is to appreciate how important they are in this digitized, fast-paced world that we are now a part of. They impact how we are perceived and valued and connect right to the attributes that we discussed earlier when I asked you to complete the statement, "People like to work with people they . . ." We established that most people want to work with people they like, trust and respect. By establishing your Credibility, Integrity and Authenticity, you become someone who people want to work with—even someone they want to share common goals with, where business relationships have the opportunity to work at the highest level.

CAPABILITY BUILDER

Think about a behavior or approach to demonstrate to a colleague the three essential qualities of Relational Capital:

1. Credibility:

_____

2. Integrity:

_____

3. Authenticity:

_____

While we all possess these qualities and each is important on its own, understanding the power of their convergence is how Relational Leaders are able to Care About People's Goals, Passions and Struggles through the Relational GPS model. Therefore, our illustration of Principle #2 is complete through our appreciation and practicing of the Essential Qualities of Relational Capital (figure 3-7).

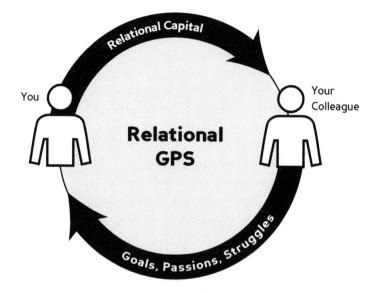

Figure 3-7. Relational GPS and Relational Capital.

Relational Leaders follow Principle #2: Care About People's Goals, Passions and Struggles as their road map to relational and business success.

Relational GPS is your universal framework for relational success!

4

PRINCIPLE #3
Make Every Interaction Matter

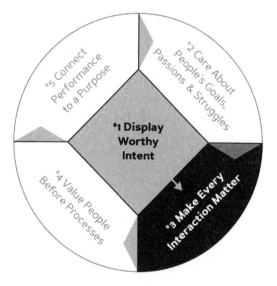

Figure 4-1. Relational Leaders make every interaction matter.

NOW THAT WE'VE SPENT some time getting acquainted with the principle of Worthy Intent and emphasizing the basic need to connect personally with the important aspects of other people regardless of generation—with Principle #2: Care About People's Goals, Passions and Struggles—we're in a position to think about how to live Principle #3: Make Every Interaction Matter, with the people we work with as well as with everyone else in some memorable way.

RELATIONAL MICRO-MOMENTS

Before the days of E-ZPass and other automated ways to collect tolls, there was a toll taker on the Golden Gate Bridge who began to think more deeply about his interactions with the commuters, and then something remarkable happened. He realized that in many cases, he was the first person that the commuters spoke to or at least interacted with each day. It struck him that he had a unique opportunity to set the tone for that person's day. He asked himself, why not turn a mundane, routine process into a memorable moment? This allowed him to enjoy his work even more, despite long hours and tough conditions, and he got a reputation for being chatty, funny and good-natured, even for being a joker. Drivers would seek out his lane—like in the supermarket checkout line with the best or fastest grocery bagger—just to interact with him for twenty seconds. His toll booth line was easy to find because it was always the longest one. Commuters would comment that they felt like they had an actual *relationship* with the toll-taker, that he was warm and felt like a friend.

Consider the impact all of this had on the thousands of commuters that went through the booth every day. How many people had better days because of these literal drive-by interactions? How far forward were those great feelings carried? At a time when we have never been more connected, but our business relationships have never been shallower, Relational Micro-moments such as these can make all the difference.

Relational Micro-moments is a term I use to cover every instance of when a business relationship has the opportunity to learn some GPS so it can be launched or advanced. Examples are:

- Interactions in the hallway with a person you have not met
- Seeing the same person in the company cafeteria every day

- Every email, phone message, text, conference call, online meeting and webinar
- Formal and informal meetings and conferences
- Interacting with the person sitting next to you on a plane
- Interacting with the person waiting in line for coffee at Starbucks
- Interacting with the person standing in the checkout line at Walmart
- Putting a team together by getting suggestions from colleagues
- Accepting a LinkedIn invitation by actually writing back and making a personal connection with the other person

Southwest Airlines: Branding Relational Micro-moments

Relational Micro-moments don't have to be strictly of the moment. Southwest Airlines, for instance, continues to grow by building these moments into their brand. I was recently flying on a competing airline of Southwest's and found myself seated next to a person whose suit must have cost a few thousand dollars. We struck up a conversation and I learned that he was the CEO of a tech company about to complete a capital raise. We talked off and on for most of the flight, and then as usually happens, we landed late and there was no gate available for us to deplane. After about thirty minutes of waiting, he said gruffly, "I really don't like flying on this airline. If it is not things like this, then their planes are late or the flight attendants are coarse."

So I asked, "Do you have a preferred airline when you have options?"

"Absolutely, Southwest!" he said.

Southwest is my favorite, but I was interested in learning why a first-class-seat kind of traveler would prefer them too, so I asked him. This opened the floodgates.

"First off, they are usually on time and scheduling is easy," he offered.

"What else?"

"Their employees are so much fun to be around!" he commented with a smile.

"Can you give me any examples?"

"Sure. On my last flight, during the safety announcements, the flight attendant joked, 'Give your seat belt a tug, give your neighbor a hug. We've got to get this Boeing going.'"

He continued . . .

"Then on another flight they got in early and then apologized, 'Welcome to Chicago, folks, and sorry, we're early!'"

We both chuckled at that.

He kept commenting . . .

"Then one time the pilot came out and we sang 'Happy Birthday' to a military service person."

"On another occasion, the flight attendants made us laugh during turbulence."

"Ed, their logo is a heart with wings, for crying out loud. That says it all."

And on and on. Needless to say this savvy business traveler preferred the experience on Southwest to the comfort of a first-class seat.

Southwest has left no stone unturned in making every interaction matter with its traveling customers, whether it be pleasant, sometimes funny gate personnel; easy boarding and deplaning; simple ways to upgrade your seat or change your flight; pleasant flight attendants; no beverage carts blocking the aisles; or pilots who keep you updated. I can appreciate this approach even more when I think about Southwest's challenge of delivering on warm "little things" to their very diverse base of flyers, which includes some businesspeople like me who travel frequently, families who travel on vacation and older people who may only fly every so often. I have traveled next to passengers who were nervous about flying and observed how the crew made the flight a bit more relaxed by sharing quips or making some lighthearted comments. By making every interaction matter, Southwest has created an experience that attracts all three of the generations that I mentioned earlier—Boomers, Gens and Millennials.

THE PROXIMITY DILEMMA

It is easy to look at an intense project or a big business partner presentation as being a platform for transformative relationships. But an outstanding business relationship can span from a simple request from a colleague. How many times in your life have you had what seemed to be a drive-by interaction with a colleague and somewhere down the road it manifested into something wonderful for both of you? The challenge today comes with proximity or lack thereof to our colleagues. Traditionally, close proximity led to the opportunity to strengthen interactions. With electronic communications taking over most of our day, we need to work even harder to communicate and collaborate with our colleagues. While face to face is still the most effective way due to all of the body language and subtle cues right in front of us, Relational Leaders consider relationships in the context of all of the potential interaction scenarios available to us as well as serving a diverse group of colleagues and stakeholders that span multiple generations as indicated earlier. Let's take a look at an organization that understands that challenge and intentionally aspires to make every interaction matter with its constituents.

Plastics Industry Association: Making Every Interaction with Plastic Matter

Bill Carteaux, president of the Plastics Industry Association, makes me feel great during and after every interaction. I asked him, "How does one set out to change perceptions of the plastics industry while growing a mostly volunteer organization?" Bill said his goal was to "ensure that everyone understands Plastics Industry Association's common goal—to serve *all* constituents who rely on the plastics industry." By "all," he means not just their members, but everyone who uses plastic: consumers, board members, Plastics Industry Association employees and their families, and legislators.

The Plastics Industry Association works every day through every interaction to overcome this challenge to deliver on its common goal through three strategic pillars: advocacy, outreach and industry growth and development.

▶ *Advocacy*

Board members who have spent their lives running their companies and helping their own employees somehow also commit significant time as volunteers, doing their best for the industry. Every issue is addressed during board meetings and in the ensuing follow-ups, which take even more time. Many members run family-owned companies and are more passionate about creating a legacy of bettering the industry, rather than financial rewards.

▶ *Outreach*

To help overcome the perceptions of plastics and pollution, real solutions are created and implemented. During each board meeting, a plenary session is conducted around, for example, recycling. To make the interaction really matter, the members will visit a recycling center and then meet with industry, academia and government to ensure the most efficient recycling programs are instituted at their companies. When the focus was marine debris, the Plastics Industry Association sponsored Operation Clean Sweep, to help all plastics companies keep resin pellets from escaping to the marine environment. The SEA Research Foundation later found an 80 percent reduction in pellet concentration, coinciding with the exact time frame of the Operation Clean Sweep Program.

▶ *Industry Growth and Development*

The Plastics Industry Association, like many member organizations, runs conferences each year where it brings members and customers together along with other industry experts, constituents and critics. During these conferences, every Plastics Industry Association employee regardless of role engages with the attendees in order to create and strengthen relationships across the board.

The Plastics Industry Association has also been a big advocate of 3-D printing, which has been around awhile but is once again changing the world with the emergence of smaller, cheaper 3-D printers. Now a wounded veteran can have a prosthesis made for a tenth of the cost and in less time—basically on demand. Within ten years, 3-D printers will be in every operating room, classroom and even car dealership, where everything from body parts to fenders can be manufactured significantly cheaper and quicker.

If you think about this technology from a green or environmental sustainability standpoint, on-demand printing saves materials because manufacturers no longer need to build and keep molds forever, and saves money with faster delivery to all kinds of customers.

Even the Plastics Industry Association office environment is a source of Relational Micro-moments. It's ironic because when I think of the word "environment," in relation to leadership, I think less of physical environment and more of mission, values, work–life balance and so forth. But with the Plastics Industry Association, it actually begins with their office environment. Bill has refitted an entire floor in Washington, DC, as if it were a plastics manufacturing facility. Starting with the vinyl flooring that looks like concrete to an open industrial ceiling to the fixtures and conference room tables, every aspect of the office reflects something manufactured or recycled in their industry. There is even background white noise that sounds like machinery running in a plant. The office theme and aesthetics allow Bill and the Plastics Industry Association to visually provide proof of the industry's commitment to overcome its challenges because he invites all kinds of constituents and non-advocates to visit through the hosting of various events. This is a great example of how true Relational Leaders positively engage with everyone connected to their goals, even potential adversaries, in order to establish Relational Capital regardless of any issues that divide them.

Finally, the Plastics Industry Association's Relationship Intentionality is further exemplified by empowering its employees with unlimited paid time off (PTO)—self-directed based on the ability to deliver on business commitments. While not a new concept, the Plastics Industry Association was an early adopter of actually implementing this approach to continue to build trust within the organization.

By the way, I mentioned earlier in this book that being intentional about relationships has a huge impact on performance and that is certainly the case with the Plastics Industry Association. Bill shared that they have quadrupled over the past ten years by intentionally seeking to make every interaction matter. It's a fact of life that we all use plastics and we all have to figure out what to do with them when we are finished.

CAPABILITY BUILDER

Think about and record three Relational Micro-moments that you believe had a big impact on someone else and why.

_____

_____

_____

Which one could you perform again tomorrow?

_____

There is opportunity in every interaction.

5

PRINCIPLE #4
Value People Before Processes

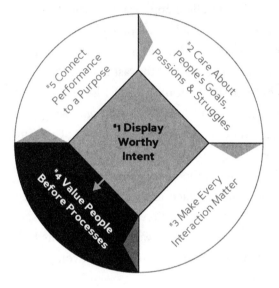

Figure 5-1. Relational Leaders value people before processes.

L IKE THE FIRST THREE principles of becoming a Relational Leader, Principle #4: Value People Before Processes plays a major role in advancing your business relationships and improving performance over time. I previously discussed how complex and process centric our companies and organizations are today. Also, in this environment, Relational Leaders are challenged with developing even more processes to help drive performance.

Unfortunately, a process, no matter how well-intentioned in its design, can fail spectacularly again and again, yet continue to be used in an organization. The prime example: cable company customer service, as I discovered when I had a problem with my box.

After listening to on-hold music for more than ten minutes and providing the last four digits of my Social three times, I now have the right person on the line to help me with my cable television problem.

"Hello, Mr. Wallace, this is Danielle. How's it going today?"

"OK, I guess, Danielle. I appreciate your getting on the line. It's nice to hear the voice of a human being!"

"No problem, Mr. Wallace, and for verification purposes, can I please have your zip code and the last four digits of your Social?"

"Sure, but this is the fourth time I have provided this info!" (Now I'm thinking, *Am I sure she's a human being?*)

"I understand completely, Mr. Wallace, but I do need the info again for verification purposes," Danielle assured me.

"OK," I responded, then gave her the numbers.

"Thank you, Mr. Wallace, and now what may I assist you with?"

"Well, as I mentioned to three of your colleagues, my cable signal is lost and we are trying to watch the big game today."

"No problem, Mr. Wallace, but I'll need you to do a few things for me."

"OK, anything at this point, Danielle. Just ask me," I replied exasperated.

"Can you please go over to your cable box and read off to me the bar code number on the bottom?"

"You mean the black box under my TV or the white box?" I asked.

"Well, it depends. Do you know your account number so I can look that up?"

Who knows their cable account number?

"Not really, but maybe I can describe the boxes that I have?" I offered.

"OK, let's try that. What does the white box say?"

"X Gear," I say.

"No, that's not the right one. What does the black box say?" Danielle engages, now determined to get to the bottom of my issue.

"You mean the one down at floor level under everything else?"

"Yes, that's the one."

"I'll have to crawl across my living room floor to get to where I can actually look at it," I comment, dismayed.

"I'm waiting."

I crawl, then contort myself so I can read the label on the box.

"Y Gear," I finally say.

"That's it! Now let's work with that one," she excitedly declares.

"OK, what's next?" I ask.

"Now, look at the underside of the Y Gear box and read off the numbers *under* the bar code to me," she directs.

"Wow, these numbers are really small!" I say. "And there are three different *sets* of numbers."

"Yes, that's correct," she says with no discernible trace of sympathy. "Now, try to find the one that begins with a *K*."

"I would, but the cables are all connected and I can't lift the box up high enough to read the numbers clearly. There's no light back here!"

"Do you have a magnifying glass or something that will allow you to view the number any better?" she says, in an effort to be helpful.

I am thinking, *REALLY? YOU ARE ASKING ME TO FIND A MAGNIFYING GLASS TO SOLVE YOUR SERVICE PROBLEM?*

And so on . . . eventually, I pushed enough buttons, wiggled enough wires, read off enough numbers, and the cable company sent enough signals through all those mysterious cable lines to finally bring the game back to life on the screen for my anxious family. But what an ordeal!

I like to share this story because if we break down this process, we find that a team of leaders at some large cable organization, who I truly want to believe had Worthy Intent, attempted to design a process to help their customers. They then trained a team of customer service representatives to ask their customers—who pay a tremendous amount of money each month—to "crawl across their living room floors" just to get back the cable service they've already paid for?

The obvious paradox is that good or even perceived Worthy Intent can manifest as a poor *experience*—there's that word again—for a customer or a colleague. Think about it; if you worked in customer service for the cable company, your engagement with customers included these types of interactions every day. I wonder how long most people could manage those kinds of conversations as part of their work experience.

THE BIGGEST PROBLEM WITH PROCESS IS PEOPLE!

As I shared in chapter 1, businesses are organized and driven by well-defined organization charts and processes. Over the years, these processes have been restructured, reengineered, remapped and whatever other "re" word you can come up with. However, in most cases the process designers have assumed that relational capital exists and will carry the performance day for the human beings involved with and interacting within the process. The challenge is that strong relationships can never be assumed. In reality, the biggest problem with any well-designed process is the failure of the process *to consider* the PEOPLE! Weakness or lack of intention in relationships will blur or confuse the sharp lines developed in company process flow charts and ultimately hamper performance. These relationships run the gamut from process envisioning, design, implementation and ultimately all the way to the customer both internal and external.

I summarized chapter 1 with the Organization 3.0 model by indicating that after everything being done with structures and processes, results still get down to strong one-to-one connections in order to avoid all of the blurred lines, perceived and real hierarchy, and unclear decision-making processes that really exist in organization charts (see figure 5-2 for a reminder).

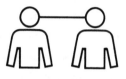

Figure 5-2. Organization 3.0: one-to-one relationship.

In this chapter, I introduce Principle #4: Value People Before Processes and how it contrasts and impacts the old "thinking outside the box" cliché. Relationship Intentionality happens between the process boxes, not outside of them. You really cannot think outside the box if you do not have strong relationships from box to box, in effect relationally. Relational Leaders are successful through the experience they create for other people. My cable experience is an example of how Relational Leadership somehow missed the mark. I mentioned Safelite's approach to Relational Leadership in the introduction of this book, and now I'd like to share how its approach has manifested in superior performance.

Safelite AutoGlass: Decide Who Comes First

Some companies put shareholders first. Some put customers first. At Safelite, CEO Tom Feeney made a conscious, intentional decision to put the company's people first, with the simple belief that happy people create happy customers who in turn deliver profitable growth. Every company must decide where to focus its disciplines and core values. Tom, his board and his leadership team bravely chose their people first using the following thinking:

- Core values are choosing who comes first: shareholders or employees or customers.
- Disciplines are choosing what comes first: operations, products or customer service.

Tom will be the first to state that there are not any wrong answers to this analysis. The critical point for any company is to ask the question and make sure its resources and processes are aligned with the answer. Companies that never answer these questions can be unfocused and often suboptimize their performance.

Therefore, Safelite's first transformation required a decision: Who comes first? The group decided on "their people," as Tom explained for this simple reason: "We believe it's a very simple equation—take care of your people and they will take care of their customers."

Next, Safelite's strategy was to transition its focus from its operational efficiency to listening more to its customers. Tom likes to say, "All of our decisions on how we operate will be driven by the customers' needs. This is how 'People Powered, Customer Driven' came to be our philosophy." Make no mistake that all companies absolutely need processes, but by deciding which comes first (and in Safelite's case, it's its people), it has achieved the following:

- Employee engagement has increased from 77 percent to 80 percent (a score of 75 percent is consistent with best in class)
- Sales increase by 174 percent
- Profitability has grown 231 percent

This brings us back to the impact of Principle #4. Relational Leaders are challenged with designing and leading processes that, by definition, involve human beings, not just boxes in a flow chart or organizational diagram. There is no question that thinking intentionally about the relationships among the team members, colleagues and other stakeholders in the process is challenging, yet the very success of the process or project is heavily *dependent* on these relationships.

CAPABILITY BUILDER

After reading about Safelite's approach to Relational Leadership, how would you have changed the process for the cable customer? What five "thinking between the boxes" ideas powered by your knowledge of the principles of Worthy Intent; caring about people's goals, passions and struggles; and make every interaction matter would you have designed into the process?

Now here are some ideas on how the cable company could align with Principle #4: Value People Before Processes:

- Put the wires on the side of the box.

- Put the serial numbers and bar codes on the front or side.

- Make the serial numbers larger.

- Offer a service call versus crawling across the floor.

- Invest in a wireless infrastructure as soon as possible.

- Enable customers to get box data from their account page on the cable company's website.

■ Enable customers to label their cable boxes online as living room, bedroom, etc., rather than by model numbers for ready reference.

As you review this list, did any of your ideas match up? A closer look at the list indicates that even the simplest idea—make the serial numbers larger—would have a huge impact on the experience that the cable company is creating for its customers. Sometimes solutions that value people first are right in front of us if we listen and pay attention to the Relational GPS coming back to us.

Relational Leaders are challenged with designing and leading processes that by definition involve human beings, not just boxes in a flow chart or organizational design. We can't afford to think only outside the process boxes, because processes will not proceed from one phase to the next without the right people and right relationships in place to drive the processes and optimize their intended results.

Relational Leaders ensure that people come before processes!

6

PRINCIPLE #5
Connect Performance to a Purpose

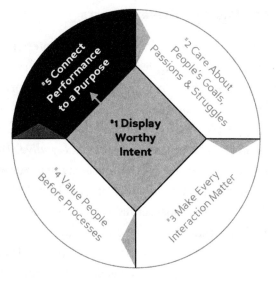

Figure 6-1. Relational Leaders connect performance to a purpose.

RELATIONAL LEADERS ALWAYS FOCUS on "why they do what they do." When it comes to relationships, the biggest challenge that they face is making sure that all of the relationships they are developing and supporting connect to some aspect of meaning and performance. Of course, this challenge is bound like everything else in life by time, everyone's most nonrenewable resource. Whenever I struggle with how I am spending my time, I challenge myself with the following five questions:

1. Who do I want to be?
2. How do I want to be perceived?
3. What am I here for?
4. What is most important to me?
5. What will my contribution be?

Here's how DaVita, a nationwide healthcare company, handles these questions.

DaVita Rx's Mission-Driven Hearts

With more than fourteen hundred dialysis centers nationwide, DaVita Corporation has countless opportunities every day to leave lasting impressions to live Principle #5: Connect Performance to a Purpose. As I drove by one of DaVita's dialysis centers recently, it struck me that people with kidney issues rely on the care, skills and equipment within each of these centers to *stay alive*. There is no margin for error; life or death could be at stake for every patient that DaVita cares for. With that daunting mission, DaVita has instilled a culture that foremost serves the patient before all else, because the further a leader gets from clinical care, the easier it could become to lose sight of individual patients and their needs. Decisions are made with patients' needs at the forefront and this has led to remarkable growth, making DaVita the largest healthcare provider in the United States. In order to further support this growth, in 2005 DaVita created its own pharmaceutical subsidiary and, not surprisingly, DaVita Rx has since grown to $1 billion in sales over those ten years with a forecast that dwarfs that number over the next ten.

When you walk into the DaVita Rx office locations, they resemble Main Street in a quaint town. There's a coffee shop area and storefronts. You don't get the sense that you're far removed from one of the dialysis centers that DaVita Rx serves in towns and cities across the United States. On top of that, the company's hierarchical structure has subdivisions with names you might find in a futuristic science-fiction novel: employees are called Citizens, the corporate office is called the Village and offices are fittingly called Neighborhoods. All of this verbally and visibly reinforces that it all begins with DaVita Rx taking care of its own employees.

In the center of a Village sits senior executive John Romer. I asked John about the key driver or lever that creates this strong growth at both the corporate and divisional levels. He said, "Our success is based on one simple, irrefutable tenet—connecting everybody's daily activities to the broader purpose of how our decisions and actions impact the well-being of our dialysis patients."

To accomplish this, DaVita Rx amplifies Principle #5: Connect Performance to a Purpose in three key ways.

First, they hire people with "mission-driven hearts," people committed to helping others in need through their Worthy Intent. "The key to finding future Citizens," John said, "is to populate the Village by being intentional about hiring relational people with industry experience who see their work as contributing to something much more than just earning a paycheck." The hiring process includes a great deal of conversations with candidates to learn about them and their potential for being a cultural fit coupled with getting feedback from the various groups they will interact with across the Village and Neighborhood. While technical and professional hard skills are a given, the ability to create a great experience for others whether they are patients or colleagues is the key to delivering on DaVita Rx's mission.

Next, they maintain a culture that aligns decision making with patient care and clinical outcomes. I learned from Chief Development Officer Lynn Robinson's senior leadership team that DaVita Rx values diverse perspectives, which leads to powerful collaborations and solutions but can also be challenging when ultimate decisions need to be made. Lynn commented, "The impact on the patient is the ultimate backboard for all decision making. We all work to ensure that decisions and the operationalization of the resulting plans align with this tenet throughout the process." A great example is something that has impacted every business in the United States—the Affordable Care Act (ACA).

While this law impacts most businesses internally, the ACA has a tremendous impact on DaVita Rx's patients as well. Leadership decided that regardless of all the political rhetoric and individuals' personal biases one way or the other regarding the legislation, the company needed to get out ahead of the healthcare overhaul and align with it even as it was still evolving. DaVita Rx owed its patients across the country this diligence. It couldn't afford to be behind or its life-saving work could be jeopardized.

Finally, DaVita Rx regularly goes beyond the company mission to make an impact on the world too—for instance, its Village Service Days.

Tyler Tuttle is a sales leader who works with Lynn and John. Tyler and I were planning a training program for one of its sales meetings, and as we were comparing calendars, he mentioned that the company could not work with me on a particular day because that was a Village Service Day. Of course I was intrigued as to what that meant. Tyler explained that whenever he brings the team together, they always invest half a day doing something meaningful well beyond their job descriptions. His comment, "You can spend all of the money in the world throwing money at problems, but that only gets you so far. If you really want to change and help others, you need to get involved personally and in person." During this meeting the team was going to visit a Boys and Girls Club in a tough neighborhood and do various tasks working with the kids to make holiday gifts for kids who were even worse off than they were. Before he could bring it up, I asked, "May I join you and the team?" He was thrilled that I would take the time to help out.

The Village Service Day not only helped me see even more of how DaVita Rx connects performance to a purpose, but personally it helped me gain balanced perspective and just a good feeling about helping others. I asked, "How do you find the time several times each year to take this many people away from customers and all that goes with that?" Of course, I was thinking of the cost to the company for these days away from partner and customer work.

"If you really want to change and help others, you need to get involved personally and in person."

Tyler simply responded, "Because it's the right thing to do. Why are we working so hard anyway if we can't find some kind of meaning beyond our paychecks?" Then he added, "Plus, it's a great team-building exercise!"

While many companies do a tremendous job extending beyond their missions through corporate-level guidance, I like highlighting DaVita's approach because it empowers leaders at the Village level to determine how best to serve their constituents.

Some might say you can't put purpose before profits. The thing is, purpose pulls profits along the way a horse pulls a cart. So it's not surprising that Tyler's team was having an outstanding sales year as of this writing!

To sum up DaVita Rx's special approach and culture, it's easy to *say* you're going to put the patient first, but living up to that promise isn't easy. Oh and by the way, from a performance standpoint DaVita Rx has grown exponentially, transforming from a billion-dollar idea into a billion-dollar reality. However, this financial gain is a mere by-product of DaVita Rx's common goal of giving patients the best possible clinical care fueled by its Citizens' "mission-driven hearts."

CAPABILITY BUILDER

Think of an opportunity where you and/or your team can connect performance to a purpose within your company or community. Decide when you will seek to deliver on this opportunity.

CONNECT PERFORMANCE TO A PURPOSE IN A BUSINESS THAT "WENT FOR" THE DOGS

One of my favorite Relational Leader stories is about Bill Smith, the founder of the Main Line Animal Rescue (MLAR). Located near historic Valley Forge outside of Philadelphia, MLAR is considered by many to be the finest animal shelter in the United States. Bill Smith started Main Line Animal Rescue over sixteen year ago in his garage, using what little he could of his own money. Please take it from a family (the Wallaces) that has adopted three dogs from Bill, he willed Main Line Animal Rescue into existence purely on sheer Worthy Intent, connecting performance to a purpose, and the power of relationships.

As I began conceptualizing this book, I wrestled with ways to best exhibit Principle #5: Connect Performance to a Purpose since I had so many choices from all of the Relational Leaders I researched and knew. Even though this book is about people and their business relationships, I thought that Bill Smith's story of how he took MLAR from a simple garage then to a barn and then to his appearance on *The Oprah Winfrey Show* as a leading advocate against animal cruelty would be most appreciated by my readers. It all began with Bill's passion for dogs and other innocent animals that find themselves in dire straits.

From their website: "Main Line Animal Rescue, located minutes from Valley Forge National Park in scenic Chester County, Pennsylvania, is considered by many to be the finest animal shelter in the United States. With more than four hundred active volunteers, thousands of animals helped every year, a state-of-the-art veterinary clinic, innovative training and educational programs, and almost sixty acres of fenced pastures and walking trails, Main Line Animal Rescue is not only a sight to behold but an experience you will never forget." All of this from a noble purpose and a garage!

Every year MLAR assists hundreds of dogs, cats and rabbits transferred to its facility from overcrowded city shelters and notorious puppy mills. Many of these animals are in need of costly and immediate medical care. Adopting families are carefully screened before animals are released to their care. MLAR even assists families who are no longer able to care for their pets for various reasons.

MLAR has been recognized nationally as a leader in the fight against puppy mill abuse. Their 2008 billboard in Chicago led to Oprah Winfrey's groundbreaking and award-winning exposé on puppy mills as well as undercover investigations by many acclaimed journalists. By 2009, their efforts with *Newsweek* led to Whole Foods Markets issuing a directive to all of their suppliers: they would no longer sell any products from farmers who also operated puppy mills. From their work by wrapping transit buses with their message on the streets of Washington, DC, to profiles in *People* magazine and features on the *Today* show, *Nightline* and Animal Planet, MLAR has come a long way in raising awareness and helping pass many new dog-protection laws.

Wow! And as you may have guessed, Bill will not take any of the credit for the amazing success that MLAR has achieved. That goes to his large staff of volunteers, to the board members and stakeholders who believed, and to the families who adopt and care for his four-legged friends. His satisfaction comes from making a difference with the time he has on this planet through the kind act of helping dogs and other pets out of turmoil and into safe and secure environments. But let's take a closer look at the impact this manifestation of Principle #5: Connect Performance to a Purpose has in the world:

- Ensuring the safety of innocent animals
- Sharing a platform for volunteerism
- Creating public advocacy
- Inspiring a sense of purpose
- Making families happy

Relational Leaders like Bill Smith who focus on the power of Worthy Intent are in a position to truly inspire a sense of purpose in those they work with. They will see the larger good of the organization, the project or the product and the importance and excitement of their own role in supporting these. People will perform at their best with a clear sense of purpose when challenged with the following five questions:

1. Who do *you* want to be?
2. How do *you* want to be perceived?
3. What are *you* here for?
4. What is most important to *you*?
5. What will *your* contribution be?

Relational Leaders make people happy and, for that matter, puppies too! By the way, from a performance standpoint, MLAR places over one thousand dogs each and every year! Personally, Bill is one of the most centered and satisfied people I know. I can't imagine why!

CAPABILITY BUILDER

Reflect on a current project or even your current role. Please describe something you are doing today and then like our friends from DaVita Rx, Bill Smith, and me, figure out how you are going to make a difference, and record it in figure 6-2.

Action/Performance	Connecting Performance to a Purpose
Providing care and medicine to dialysis patients	Ensuring people's lives are the number one priority
Rescuing dogs and cats	Changing the world through a passion for pets
Writing a book about business relationships	Helping people serve others
Your Project:	

Figure 6-2. Examples of connecting performance to a purpose.

What will your purpose be?

PART I EXECUTIVE SUMMARY

Relational Leader Insights

- The new value proposition for leaders: Relational Leaders' success comes through the experience they create for others!
- Relational Capital is the value created by people in a business relationship.
- Three key beliefs of the Relational Leader:
  - Your success involves compelling daily interactions with people.
  - The strength of your relationships is not accidental.
  - Everybody is really smart today so relationship advancement is your last competitive distinguisher.
- Worthy Intent is the inherent promise you make to put the other person's best interests at the core of your business relationship.
- Trust is the inevitable consequence of Worthy Intent; that is, people only trust you *after* you demonstrate through your actions that you have their best interests at heart.
- Relational GPS is the road map to relational success. Relational Leaders understand that by learning the goals, passions and struggles of their colleagues and contacts they have a significantly better chance to evolve the business relationship in pursuit of common goals.
- Learning and applying Relational GPS is a simple, universal framework that allows Relational Leaders to cross generations and bridge any relational gaps between Boomers, Gens and Millennials.
- Relational Micro-moments are discrete relational opportunities to learn about the other person or just to help them have a better day.

- Treating every interaction as if you are in person increases the opportunity for a relationship to launch despite barriers caused by a lack of proximity.
- You really cannot think outside the box if you do not have strong relationships "between the organizational chart boxes"—in effect, relationally.
- Remember that many of the relationships required to ensure effective processes are At-Will—discretionary relationships that are needed to accomplish objectives.

Relational Leaders reflect and act on the following five questions when connecting performance to a purpose:

1. Who do I want to be?
2. How do I want to be perceived?
3. What am I here for?
4. What is most important to me?
5. What will my contribution be?

ULTIMATE CAPABILITY BUILDER

Reflect on the Five Principles of the Relational Leader and write down the name of a person who you believe best exemplifies each principle:

Display Worthy Intent: _____

Care About People's GPS: _____

Make Every Interaction Matter: _____

Value People Before Processes: _____

Connect Performance to a Purpose: _____

RELATIONAL AGILITY: HARNESSING THE POWER OF WORTHY INTENT

7

THE RELATIONAL AGILITY PROCESS
Navigating the Complexity

HOW DO YOU BECOME *a Relational Leader?* This chapter introduces the Relational Agility Process and sets the foundation for how to use it to apply the Five Principles to your important business relationships. In *Business Relationships That Last*, I introduced a process called the Relational Ladder (figure 7-1) to illustrate how someone in business development or other customer-facing roles can advance a prospect or client relationship from being an acquaintance to becoming a respected adviser— ultimately in pursuit of the goal of creating great relationships in support of sales goals. Here's a quick refresher because, after all, Relational Leaders are all in sales—influencing around their ideas and recommendations.

Advancing business relationships can be achieved through a repeatable process called the Relational Ladder. To date, over twenty-five thousand business professionals have learned about and made use of the Relational Ladder in their daily work flow to transform their relationships from acquaintances to respected advisers.

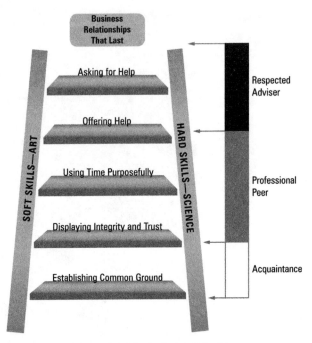

Figure 7-1. The Relational Ladder.

As you can see, the Relational Ladder has five rungs or steps:

1. Establishing Common Ground—launch the relationship
2. Displaying Integrity and Trust—secure the relationship
3. Using Time Purposefully—invest in the relationship
4. Offering Help—share relational equity
5. Asking for Help—realizing returns on your investment

These five steps represent a repeatable process for business relationship advancement that allows you to build strong enough relationships to balance your hard- and soft-skill tendencies and take you from an acquaintance to a professional peer to ultimately a respected adviser. The end result is an easy way to create strategies for customer relationships and proactively think about where you need to take a relationship to help the customer accomplish their goals with your needs being met in the process.

Note: Please refer to the Relational Ladder Abstract from *Business Relationships That Last* in the appendix of this book for more specifics on how to use the Relational Ladder to build customer-focused relationships.

In management and leadership, the dynamic, of course, is somewhat more challenging. I mentioned in chapter 1 that Relational Leaders work in a complex relationship environment, with combinations or synapses that make their potential At-Will relationships almost look like molecules when you factor in the matrix, hierarchical and external relationships they navigate daily. I also mentioned that Relational Leaders can be anyone, not solely sales professionals or executives, so we need to consider a broader set of principles and processes for success because you need to collaborate differently with a customer than you do when you combine colleagues, team members, executives, suppliers and customers.

However, before we get too far along with the Relational Agility Process, which is all about an intentional way to build relationships as we collaborate together, I first want to clarify what the word "collaborate" actually means. Sometimes we go along in our careers and hear words that we just accept without fully understanding or exploring their meaning. The word "quality" comes to mind because "quality" is really defined based on the needs of the person seeking something of that quality. For example, quality to an art collector may be very different than quality to a person who shops in a discount store. "Collaborate" is one of those words like "quality" that has many meanings and interpretations. Many companies and technology tool builders throw "collaborate" out there as a sophisticated way for us to work or how they can help us work through complex collaborations.

The fact is that "to collaborate" means simply "to work together with a person or group to achieve something." Therefore, effective collaborations tie directly to sharing common goals, which connects with the findings from chapter 1 where relationships work at the highest level when people share these. So now let's begin by first learning about an approach for categorizing your relationships as you collaborate.

DIMENSIONALITY

In my collaborations with clients and specifically at their request to meet leadership development needs, I have evolved the Relational Ladder process so that Relational Leaders can apply it to their very own collaborations using a dimensional perspective. The focus in the Relational Agility Process is on three dimensions that Relational Leaders need to navigate and plan for, using the principle of Worthy Intent versus going from step to step in ascending the Relational Ladder with customers (see figure 7-2).

Instead of entering the business relationship at the acquaintance level, you will generally be entering in a defined or at least perceived hierarchical relationship, with others either below or above you in the organization or at a similar level. Also, since complex, cross-functional matrix-based organizations have flattened the impact of hierarchy, creating At-Will business relationships as we mentioned earlier, I simply call the first dimension Colleagues. The nature of this defined relationship will determine how you approach improving it. Developing business relationships with your superiors may be similar in some ways to working on developing prospects into clients. Working with peers or direct reports will be much more a question of developing mutual trust and respect, overcoming distrust of your position or motives—with the goal of creating and maintaining genuine influence—and transforming your working relationships into strong collaborations.

The next dimension in the Relational Agility Process is called Professional Peers—business relationships that allow Relational Leaders to work together without concern for hierarchy or perceived organizational power. You may have noticed that Professional Peers is a dimensional term from the Relational Ladder as well, but it holds even stronger applications for Relational Leaders who need even more Intentionality due to technological distances and cross-functional team roles. Professional Peers is the targeted category for most business relationships to be successful.

The third dimension is creating such strong business relationships that Relational Leaders win over colleagues and team members as Advocates—those who support or promote the interests of another—for your ideas and the company's goals. Advocate-level relationships can be aspirational or real depending on the situation and performance goals involved. This table summarizes these three types of At-Will dimensions:

Colleagues	Know each other or simply acknowledge they work for the same organization, but may not have worked on common goals previously.
Professional Peers	Advanced business relationship around common goals where there is no perceived role/hierarchy when working together.
Advocates	Career-spanning relationships that exceed the scope of the common goals previously worked on. Highest-level business relationship where Relational Leaders support each other's best interests beyond the situation.

Figure 7-2. Dimensions of the Relational Agility Process.

Frank Coates, CEO of Wheelhouse Analytics, used a metaphor to explain this dimensionality of coworkers quite clearly. Frank has a way about him that allows him to cut right to the point clearly and definitively. He said, "Let's think about it in terms of moving from an apartment or house. Imagine you have a deadline, your movers have engine trouble and you need help. You have three friends you believe that you have strong relationships with so you ask them for help."

Your first friend says, "Sorry, I'm busy, maybe some time later in the week." She's a Colleague.

Your next friend says, "Sure, I can squeeze it in after the game." He's a Professional Peer.

Your third friend drops everything, comes right over and brings pizza. He's an Advocate.

While to some extent these may seem extreme or absolute, they establish an easy-to-remember metaphor for understanding the parameters around the dimensions.

Now, let's think about this in terms of a business project and it is 5:00 p.m. You just learned that you have a forecast due by 7:00 p.m. because your boss has a board meeting tomorrow. As you are watching everyone leave the office you begin to ask for help.

- Your Colleague apologizes but has to leave.
- Your Professional Peer says she can help tomorrow.
- Your Advocate cancels her dinner plans.

The key point is not that Colleague relationships are necessarily worse compared with Professional Peer and Advocate relationships. It is that we will need all three to harness the power of Worthy Intent in our At-Will relationships. *The key is that each dimension can be appropriate, even strategic, based on the goals we are trying to accomplish.* I would not expect a Colleague to just drop everything to help with the project since they have not allocated time and were not aware of my need. However, as you will see here in Part II, Colleague relationships are valuable when launched effectively through the connection to common goals. In similar fashion, the need to advance to stronger Professional Peer and Advocate relationships is situational based on the goals required.

CAPABILITY BUILDER

Write down your goals for the next twelve months and connect your important business relationships to the dimension you believe is required to accomplish each goal:

Goal	Important Business Relationship	Dimension (Colleague, Professional Peer, Advocate)

Figure 7-3 Dimensions of Accomplishing Goals

Based on your results, prioritize and list below the top three relationships that will require the most relational capital investment and how you will address them.

_____

_____

_____

GROUPS OF PEOPLE ARE DIFFERENT

Next let's go back to thinking about the different generations of people who make up companies today. While there are many subsets, I shared previously that I like to divide them into three groups (Boomers, Gens and Millennials), each represented by a symbol, to represent my view of how they like to work in general:

If you then reflect on our models from chapter 1, we recognize that all three generations are working within most companies today. You'll recall from my Organization 2.0 model, where each generation maps into the model (figure 7-4):

Figure 7-4. Organization 2.0.

Now let's take a deeper view into some perceptions of each generation depicted in the model:

<Δ> **Boomers:** children of the "great generation" are like the oldest child in that everything was about their world until other kids came along; comfortable with the triangle (grew up in the hierarchy); they had to learn to transition and adapt to the matrix and cross-functional work; may be thinking

about retiring; working at a different pace; managing people and concerned about them; in many cases looking for ways to hang in there for another few productive years.

<≈> **Gens:** just like the middle child between the firstborn and baby of the family; looking to advance to fill some of the gaps left by retiring Boomers; maybe feeling held back because the Boomers hung in there so long; needing to pay attention to both Boomers and Millennials because of the sheer numbers in those categories; they are comfortable with distributed or cross-functional work.

<#> **Millennials:** the youngest child; show up everywhere in the triangle and parallel lines; "Generation Me"; hierarchy and teams do not bother them; could be best equipped to succeed in the new undefined world we work in; soon to be the majority of the workforce; internet savvy; electronic culture; not concerned about hierarchical titles, will text or email the CEO with no fear; may be the best equipped to handle the future.

Now let's expand our dimensions of the Relational Agility Process table to include the summary of the three generations of At-Will relationships, in figure 7-5:

Colleagues Δ ≈ #	Know each other or simply acknowledge working for the for the same organization, but may not have worked on common goals previously.
Professional Peers Δ ≈ #	Advanced business relationship around common goals where there is no perceived role/hierarchy when working together.
Advocates Δ ≈ #	Career-spanning relationships that exceed the scope of the common goals previously worked on. Highest-level business relationship where Relational Leaders support each other's best interests beyond the situation.

Figure 7-5. Dimensions of the Relational Agility Process: At-Will Generations.

THE RELATIONAL AGILITY PROCESS

Here's how the Five Principles can become part of a repeatable process with standard nomenclature for leaders and organizations to become more intentional about their business relationships. Figure 7.6 captures the principles and dimensions into a process design that can be used for Relational Leaders as they develop strategies and action plans for every business relationship.

Relational Agility Process is a process that Relational Leaders use to harness the power of Worthy Intent so they fluidly conduct collaborative interactions regardless of role, status or generation.

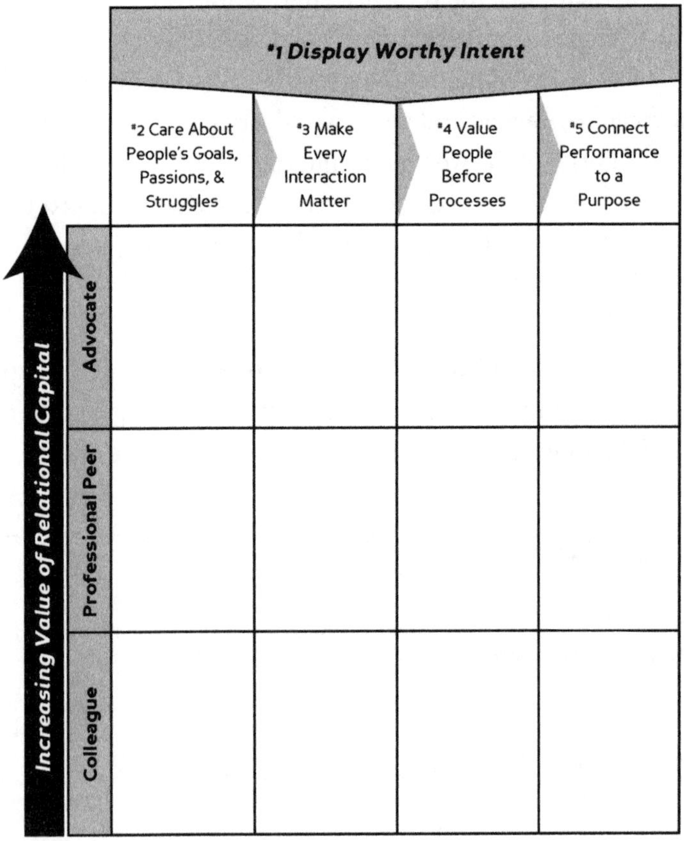

	#1 Display Worthy Intent			
	#2 Care About People's Goals, Passions, & Struggles	#3 Make Every Interaction Matter	#4 Value People Before Processes	#5 Connect Performance to a Purpose
Advocate				
Professional Peer				
Colleague				

Increasing Value of Relational Capital

Figure 7-6. Relational Agility Process.

You will notice from the Relational Agility Process that Relational Capital increases as the Relational Leader moves through the dimensions. Relational Leaders use the Relational Agility Process intentionally and situationally. Although they must master the principles as capabilities, all of the principles are not required to launch, advance or elevate every business relationship. Relational Leaders need to connect relationships intentionally to their goals and do not need to aspire to create Advocates with everyone. Realistically, Relational Leaders do not have time to take every At-Will relationship to the Advocate dimension. In fact, Advocates can be rare and almost career spanning so they may not have to be hierarchical; in fact, many times it is more effective when Advocate dimension relationships are not hierarchical, because of the nature of collaboration today laterally within organizations.

Now that we have set up the Relational Agility Process, let's begin learning how to use it by getting back to that favorite word of how we all need to work together, "collaboration."

COLLABORATION MUST START WITH GOALS

As we begin to dive into the Relational Agility Process, let's keep in mind that business performance is the key driver behind it. I have learned over the years that great Relational Leaders connect goals to actual people—not teams, not accounts, not boards, but real humans. While this idea may not seem complicated, fewer than 5 percent of leaders do it.

Let's first reflect on the fundamental beliefs from chapter 1 and our Organization 3.0 model:

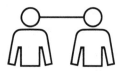

Figure 7-7. Organization 3.0: one-to-one relationship.

- Your success involves compelling daily interactions with people.
- The strength of your relationships is not accidental.
- Since everybody is really smart today, relationship advancement is your last competitive distinguisher.

We need to work with other humans to accomplish our goals, but as I shared, we tend to avoid planning or being intentional in that regard. If Relational Leaders' success is achieved through the experience they create for others, then this subtle yet powerful idea fuels a Relational Leader's success. With that in mind, there are four easy-to-follow steps that bring all of this together for aspiring Relational Leaders.

THE FOUR STEPS OF INTENTIONALITY

Here are the four steps that allow Relational Leaders to be successful with their business relationships across companies, organizational structures, countries and generations:

1. Determine your goals.
2. Attach goals to real people and their relationship dimension.

3. Develop strategies for each relationship.

4. Implement by using the Relational Agility Process for launching, advancing or elevating your important business relationships (IBRs).

Determine Your Goals

In order to make this how-to part of the book actionable, let's begin with a simulated case about an aspiring Relational Leader named Jason who will be focusing on various business relationships connected to his goals.

Jason's development plan goals for this year require him to accomplish the following:

- Transition one of his team leadership roles by the end of the first quarter
- Integrate new product from strategic alliance partner into pipeline by the end of the second quarter
- Seek executive committee approval for unbudgeted $1 million investment

Attach Goals to Real People and Their Relationship Dimension

Now that we have Jason's goals, let's determine who exactly he needs to launch, advance, or elevate relationships with to accomplish them. This is absolutely critical because, as I mentioned, most leaders today do not think about this subtlety or Intentionality when planning to accomplish their goals or objectives. So in Jason's case here are the important business relationships (IBRs) by demographic connected to his goals:

Jason's Goals	IBR	Demographic	Colleague, Professional Peer, Advocate
Transition one of his team leadership roles by the end of the first quarter	Ashley	#	Colleague
Integrate new product from strategic alliance partner into pipeline by the end of the second quarter	José	Δ	Professional Peer
Seek executive committee approval for unbudgeted $1 million investment	Beth	≈	Advocate

Note, while subtle, Jason is making a conscious, intentional decision on the specific human being (aka relationship) required to support the accomplishment of each goal.

Next, Jason needs to think about—strategize, actually—the type of relationship he needs with each of his IBRs in order to accomplish his goals. Therefore, Intentionality continues with which dimension Jason believes he will need to develop the relationship for or assign to each one.

As you can see in the table and in the summary below, Jason has determined based on the specific goal and his actual time available to invest in the Relational Capital needed for the relationship that he needs the following type of relationships:

- Ashley as a Colleague
- José as a Professional Peer
- Beth as an Advocate

Jason is making an intentional decision/conscious choice regarding his relationship strategies for accomplishing his goals. He recognizes that, based on the intensity of each goal along with the amount of time he actually has to invest, these dimensions should allow him to be successful. Imagine how much easier your work could be if you took the time to intentionally think about relation-ships as you planned your goals each year!

Now that we have set up the basis for Jason's Relational Agility action plan, he will apply the Relational Agility Process to Steps 3 and 4 of Intentionality as discussed in chapters 8 through 10 at the dimensional level:

3. Develop strategies for each relationship.

4. Implement by using the Relational Agility Process for launch-ing, advancing and elevating important business relationships (IBRs).

Every successful business relationship begins with and shares common goals.

8

LAUNCHING BUSINESS RELATIONSHIPS WITH COLLEAGUES

#1 Display Worthy Intent			
#2 Care About People's Goals, Passions, & Struggles	#3 Make Every Interaction Matter	#4 Value People Before Processes	#5 Connect Performance to a Purpose
✓	✓		

Figure 8-1. Relational Agility Process: Colleagues.

So how do we go about launching a business relationship? While it may feel daunting to some, launching a business relationship with a Colleague is a straightforward approach that aligns with the Relational Agility Process and follows these steps in relation to the first three principles:

1. Lead with a warm approach initially to display Worthy Intent.

2. Ask great questions to develop Credibility to uncover and care about GPS.
3. Use time purposely as the best way to make every interaction matter.

As you may have noticed, I enjoy sharing stories and anecdotes to help introduce or explain various concepts. So let's take a look at how the characters from the movie *Tommy Boy* apply Principle #2: Care About People's Goals, Passions and Struggles, demonstrating that comedy can actually help us learn how to launch great business relationships.

This movie premiered in 1995 and featured the late Chris Farley and his friend and partner in the movie, comedian David Spade. Chris and David's characters are named Tommy and Richard, respectively. There is a scene that really drives home the idea of Principle #2: Care About People's Goals, Passions and Struggles. They just had an awful day trying to build business relationships with customers and prospects and are debriefing in a diner. Tommy casually orders chicken wings from the server and she says, "Kitchen is closed until dinner. No hot food right now." Tommy is dismayed, asks a second time and then after being denied, he says he will just have a sugar packet. His approach was not very warm!

Tommy then approaches the server again. "Hey, what's your name?" She responds, "Helen," looking like that is the first time anyone ever cared to ask her name.

Tommy suggests that he and Helen are both in a rut and goes on to share how he is doing terribly and that they need to stick together. Helen miraculously suggests that she will personally turn the fryers back on for his chicken wings.

When I share this movie clip with my audiences and ask what caused this transformation from a definite no to a yes along with the inconvenience of the yes to Helen, I hear:

- Tommy's warm approach made it about Helen and not his goals
- Tommy found common ground around both of their plights
- Tommy made Helen feel empathetic toward him

Their responses indicated that as they looked beyond the pure comedy, they observed very real Relational Capital concepts and one-to-one connections between the characters based on the two drivers for understanding and ultimately displaying Worthy Intent from chapter 2:

1. The thoughtfulness to put others' goals ahead of your own
2. The ability to assess the behaviors of the other person

Let's break these down. Tommy quickly realized that Helen mattered as a person and began focusing on the relationship even though it would be brief based on her standoffish behavior around getting him chicken wings. He eventually stopped thinking about his own needs and warmly delivered on Principle #1: Display Worthy Intent by learning and caring about Helen's goals, passions and struggles (Principle #2). Starting with asking her name, an unlikely first from any other customer, to creating common ground about their professions and challenging plights, without asking a second time, *his* goal was actually met. While the focus above was on Worthy Intent, Principle #2: Care About People's Goals, Passions and Struggles also comes into play. Remember, Relational Leaders' success comes through the experience they create for others. Tommy created an experience focused on Helen that actually moved her *to help him.* That is the result that Relational Leaders attain as they go about promoting, dare I say selling, their ideas around their organizations.

We are talking about human beings and their complex personas so while the principles appear linear they are actually systemic and can occur simultaneously, as they did with Tommy and Helen. For now, let's agree that Worthy Intent has been accomplished and it is time to explore how to be purposeful about Principle #2: Care About People's Goals, Passions and Struggles.

You may recall that Relational Capital consists of three essential qualities—Credibility, Integrity and Authenticity (figure 8-2). The sooner we can apply these qualities when we launch a business relationship the better chance we have to learn GPS and create real Colleague relationships.

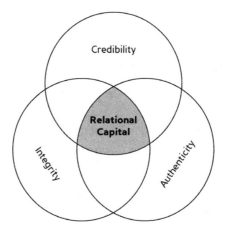

Figure 8-2. Essential Qualities of Relational Capital.

So now let's begin with Jason's first goal:

Transition one of his team leadership roles by the end of the first quarter

Jason needs to launch a relationship with Ashley, a Millennial, who works for the same company but who he has never met. Jason takes the time to assess things and decides that based on the scope and impact of his goal that a Colleague relationship is the best dimension for this emerging At-Will relationship (fig 8-3).

Goal	IBR	Demographic	Colleague, Professional Peer, Advocate
Transition one of his team leadership roles by the end of the first quarter	Ashley	#	Colleague

Figure 8-3. Jason's Business Relationship Assessment: Colleague.

Next, Jason needs to find a way to connect with Ashley around her GPS when they meet, so if we remember that the business relationship does not begin until a colleague shares his/her GPS and that first impressions are critical, Jason should consider any or all of the following ten ways for launching business relationships with Colleagues.

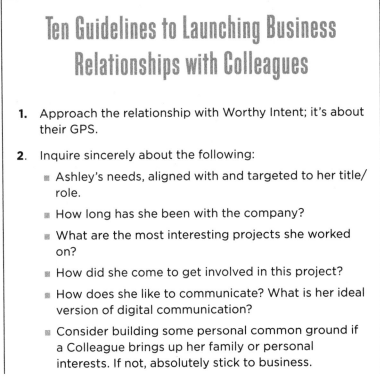

Ten Guidelines to Launching Business Relationships with Colleagues

1. Approach the relationship with Worthy Intent; it's about their GPS.

2. Inquire sincerely about the following:

   - Ashley's needs, aligned with and targeted to her title/role.
   - How long has she been with the company?
   - What are the most interesting projects she worked on?
   - How did she come to get involved in this project?
   - How does she like to communicate? What is her ideal version of digital communication?
   - Consider building some personal common ground if a Colleague brings up her family or personal interests. If not, absolutely stick to business.

(continued)

3. Resist the urge to offer solutions too early in the process.

4. Talk less, ask about goals and aspirations, listen more and care about the answers.

5. Understand business issues.

6. Make appropriate commitments and then deliver on them.

7. Document the key points of everything including GPS.

8. Set up the next meeting.

9. Prepare to discuss relevant information and questions on all follow-ups.

10. Create an action plan as a way to focus on the relationship first.

CAPABILITY BUILDER

Record behaviors you have experienced when launching successful business relationships with Colleagues. What in your approach prompted these behaviors/responses?

Colleague Behavior	Approach

APPLYING PRINCIPLE #2

In a compelling article about generational alignment, management expert Aubrey Daniels says:

> [Y]ou will come to find the critical secret to managing across generations, which is really no secret—just the science of behavior and its availability to all. Managers must simply apply the tools and principles of the science to achieve positive outcomes from all employees. Sure, it's important to encourage understanding between employees of different generations so as to avoid tensions and misconceptions. But ultimately, the best strategy for managing across the generational gap is to provide a universal framework that encourages positive behavior.[1]

Principle #2: Care About People's Goals, Passions and Struggles is a "generationally independent" approach and from a relationship standpoint the universal framework similar to what Daniels refers to above that applies to everyone regardless of their age and generation. I like to compare the idea of really knowing someone through their Relational GPS versus knowing about them to going to a movie. In its purest form a movie needs to connect with every individual in the theater. While Hollywood marketing people like to target large groups of moviegoers, ultimately the movie must connect with each individual viewer. The same thinking applies to Relational GPS as we are trying to connect with one unique human being.

CAPABILITY BUILDER

Here's a profoundly simple but effective shortcut to keep track of everything about your important business relationships so that you can align them with their Relational GPS. Prior to your next interaction, recall *one* personal and *one* business aspect of your previous meeting/discussion.

Important Business Relationship

▪ Personal aspect of previous interaction:

_____

▪ Business aspect of previous interaction:

_____

If this person likes to engage in rapport, then launch into the discussion with a question on the personal aspect. If they like to get right down to business, launch with an inquiry about the business topic.

APPLYING PRINCIPLE #3

After Jason displayed Worthy Intent and learned about Ashley's GPS during our simulation, he next should consider how to apply Principle #3: Make Every Interaction Matter when working with his Colleague Ashley.

There are many ways for Jason to apply Principle #3, but I like to focus on everyone's most valuable and nonrenewable resource—time. Besides being human the other aspect that we all have in common is having 168 hours in a week (7 × 24). Most people will comment that "I just wish I had more time," when it comes to family and work and the balance that is required. Relational Leaders recognize that each person they collaborate with has the same challenges with time as they do, with most of that time spent in meetings.

"Meetings" Is an Eight-Letter Word

Therefore, while there are countless ways prior to and after learning about your Colleague's Relational GPS to make every interaction matter, since Relational Leaders and most business professionals spend a significant amount of time in meetings, I recommend a focus on that eight-letter word that many of us dread because they are so poorly planned and executed. While this book is not simply about effective meetings it is my favorite one to focus on based on research that indicates we spend a great deal of ineffective time in meetings with our Colleagues.

According to EffectiveMeetings.com, meetings dominate our work life. In fact, approximately 11 million meetings occur in the United States every day. Although many of us complain about meetings, we can all expect to spend our careers deeply immersed in them. Most professionals attend a total of 61.8 meetings per month and research indicates that over 50 percent of this meeting time is wasted. Assuming each of these meetings is one hour long, professionals lose 31 hours per month in unproductive meetings, or approximately four workdays.

The research goes on to indicate that most professionals who meet on a regular basis admit to daydreaming (91 percent), missing meetings (96 percent) or missing parts of meetings (95 percent).

Here's my assessment of how we spend our time at work:

- 60 percent meetings
- 30 percent email
- 10 percent getting stuff done

Does this seem familiar to you?

CAPABILITY BUILDER

Think about and record how adversely ineffective meetings can impact your organization, and then compare to the list that follows:

_____

_____

From research provided by EffectiveMeetings.com, some direct effects of unproductive meetings include:

- Meetings are longer, less efficient and generate fewer results
- More meetings are needed to accomplish objectives
- With so much time spent in ineffective meetings, employees have less time to get their own work done
- Ineffective meetings create frustration at all staff levels
- Information generated in unproductive meetings usually isn't managed properly

In summary, poorly planned, designed and executed meetings cost companies billions each year in unproductive employee time. In fact, when I ask my clients about their meetings, I have yet to hear, *"We're great at holding meetings around here!"* Therefore, since Relational Leaders and their Colleagues spend so much time in meetings, I engineered a three-step process for effective meetings. Regardless of your dimension (Colleague, Professional Peer, Advocate) in the relationship or level in a company, regardless of generation, you will need to lead and attend meetings as part of your collaborations. So while we can't change the world for the better in that regard, we can make our own meetings more productive as a way of making every interaction matter.

POP EVERY MEETING INTERACTION

When planning client meetings, I think about the acronym "POP," which stands for purpose, outcomes and process. These are the three repeatable steps you can use in planning and then collaborating around every single meeting you will ever schedule. Using POP actually makes meetings easier to plan and conduct, and it helps you track and follow up on the commitments made during any given meeting.

Purpose: What and Why

The first step, *P*, or purpose, involves defining the reasons for the meeting. It answers the "what" and "why" aspects of the meeting: to describe the specific work to be completed (what), and to describe the benefits to the participants when the work is completed (why).

Worthy Intent plays a key role here because by keeping your Colleague or the group's best interests in the forefront for calling the meeting, it will be easier for you to determine who should attend or whether to even call the meeting.

I mentioned earlier that we hold meetings for many reasons, the least of which is that a meeting was already scheduled, so we might as well hold it. You will save yourself and your Colleagues many time cycles when you use a purpose statement to frame upcoming meeting interactions. A great rule of thumb: If your purpose statement cannot clearly describe the "what" and "why" for the intended meeting, reconsider calling the meeting. By thinking along these lines, you will conserve your company's and your own most non-renewable resource: time.

CAPABILITY BUILDER

For an upcoming meeting, record the following:

"What" are we trying to accomplish?

_____

"Why" will the participants benefit from participating?

_____

Outcomes: Takeaways

Now that you have developed a strong purpose statement, the next step is to plan the takeaways, the *O*, or outcomes, that each participant will leave the meeting with and concurrently determine who exactly should participate in the meeting. If you invest the time to determine the takeaways up front, then the participant list is much easier to develop. For example, if the purpose for the meeting is to provide an update on a prototype project's status, then you should be able to readily identify the team members who most need this information.

Once you have drafted the intended meeting outcomes, review it to make sure it supports the "what" and "why" in the purpose and also the takeaways you desire the participants to leave with. For example:

- Will everyone have a shared understanding of these takeaways?
- Will various participants understand what they need to do (their role, responsibilities, next steps) when the meeting concludes?
- Are the takeaways reasonable, or are they overly ambitious for the time allotted?

My personal rule is *never more than three outcomes*; more than three is too difficult to facilitate and for the group to process.

Planning your meeting outcomes will save you and your Colleagues time, help you both determine the right mix of professionals to attend the meeting and continue to distinguish yourself as a Relational Leader throughout the process.

CAPABILITY BUILDER

Think about the next meeting you are leading and develop up to three outcomes:

Meeting Title:

_____

Outcomes:

1. _____

2. _____

3. _____

Process: Meeting Agenda

This second *P*, process, represents the actual steps your meeting will follow to achieve the purpose and outcomes. The typical meeting agenda includes a list of bulleted discussion points that the participants do not get through because of poor planning and meeting facilitation. The points covered are not always captured and followed up on, while the other points drift about aimlessly intended to be covered in future meetings. Most meetings fail to make it through their agenda points and, if they do, the topics are covered only at a surface level. This second *P* takes the meeting discussion points and uses an actual process to guarantee that they are covered, and appropriately so, within the time allocated. Some example steps are included in the sample POP model that follows.

The POP Approach
- Purpose Statement ("what" are we trying to do and "why"?)
  - To ... (clearly state what we are meeting over)
  - So that ... (clearly state why people will benefit from attending)
- Outcomes/Takeaways (maximum of three)
- Process (agenda)
  - Steps for accomplishing the purpose and outcomes

Sample POP for the Next Meeting with Ashley

Let's say it's Monday, and you and Ashley have an important team transition meeting scheduled for Thursday afternoon, yet no one has taken responsibility for the meeting plan. One surefire way to create Relational Capital with Ashley is to take ten minutes and use POP to design the meeting. Send the draft process to her, seeking her input. When the process is finalized, provide all meeting participants with a copy of it.

To help you learn how easy it is for you to put this into practice in your workplace, I've created the three steps of a POP for this meeting with Ashley.

Purpose
- To continue team leader transition meetings with the project team so that the team can continue its momentum toward the project deadlines

Outcomes
- Shared understanding of the status of transition
- Identify open items for bringing the process to a close
- Next steps

Process

- Update on commitments from previous meeting (meeting leader)
- Introduce specific meeting topic—status of transition (Ashley, topic leaders)
- Dialogue on topic (group)
- Capture any agreements and/or commitments on the topic (note taker)
- Introduce next meeting topic—open items to close process (team member)
- Repeat dialogue and capture steps above
- Arrive at a path forward (meeting leader)
- Close meeting within promised time period (meeting leader)
- Document team agreements and participant commitments and launch next meeting with an update on these for continuity

CAPABILITY BUILDER

Refer to the POP template in chapter 11 to complete a meeting plan for an important upcoming meeting—consider scheduling at ten minutes past the hour.

▶ *Relational Leaders Schedule Their Meetings at Ten Minutes Past the Hour*

Whenever I suggest that you schedule your meetings at say 2:10, I get blank stares from my clients, until I ask them, where will your Colleague likely be at 2:00? I hear, "Wrapping up her previous meeting." Precisely. How can she possibly make it to your meeting when she is leaving her last meeting, maybe needing a break or time to stop by her work area to pick up some materials for your meeting?

The fun part is that she will likely ask, "Why did you schedule at 2:10?" Then you get to explain to her as I did above. Demonstrating how much you value her time with this idea goes right to the warmth and value placed on making every interaction matter that we have been discussing throughout this book. Remember Southwest's approach to looking at every interaction?

Jason's Planning

Relational Leaders plan for their important business relationships by creating an easy, straightforward action plan to accomplish their relational and business goals. Here's a sample of Jason's using a tool called the Relational Agility Action Planner (figure 8-4):

IBR	Role	
Ashley	Project Manager	
Desired Relationship Status		
☑ Colleague	☐ Professional Peer	☐ Advocate
Goal Connecting Me with IBR?	**What Is My Relationship Strategy?**	
Transition team leadership by the end of the first quarter	Strengthen Colleague dimension relationship through better understanding Ashley's GPS; plan meetings using POP process	
Goals	**Passions**	**Struggles**
Advance career to become a director in the project management function	To be determined	Getting more of a flexible schedule to watch her son play baseball in the afternoons
Key Points (Reminders for Jason)		
Ashley is a Millennial; young family; husband travels; balance is challenging; FIND WAYS TO SUPPORT THIS WHEN WORKING WITH ASHLEY		

Figure 8-4. Jason's Relational Agility Action Planner for Ashley.

Jason determined the relationship dimension required to accomplish the objective, located Ashley's Relational GPS, developed a strategy to achieve a stronger Colleague status and recorded some key personal info that should help him create a strong Colleague relationship with Ashley.

Action Planning Is Not for Everyone

I am not suggesting that you create Relational Agility action plans for every business relationship, just the relationships connected to your performance goals. This Relational Agility Action Planner tool is included in the Relational Leader toolkit in chapter 11 and can be found under Resources at www.relationalcapitalgroup.com. Please keep it handy whenever you launch a new Colleague relationship and hang on to it as you go through your career, as you never know when you may be working with Ashley again; in fact, at some point you may need to advance the relationship with Ashley for another project.

Now that we have firmly established how to launch business relationships with Colleagues, I will share how to continue turning the Five Principles into action by taking Jason's next goal through the Relational Agility Process in chapter 9: "Advancing Relationships with Professional Peers."

Launching Colleague relationships with warmth will take you a long way!

9

ADVANCING RELATIONSHIPS WITH PROFESSIONAL PEERS

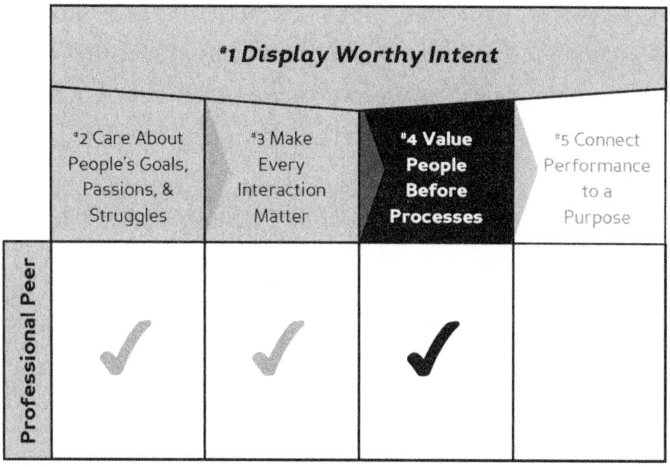

	*2 Care About People's Goals, Passions, & Struggles	*3 Make Every Interaction Matter	*4 Value People Before Processes	*5 Connect Performance to a Purpose
Professional Peer	✓	✓	✓	

*Note: The table above is headed by a banner reading "*1 Display Worthy Intent".*

Figure 9-1. Relational Agility Process: Professional Peer.

THIS CHAPTER IS ALL about how Professional Peers exercise their Relational Agility during collaborations to become Relational Leaders. The Relational Agility Process will illustrate that Professional Peer relationships will build off the Relational Capital invested from earlier displays of Worthy Intent and the application of Principle #2: Care About People's Goals, Passions and Struggles and Principle #3: Make Every Interaction Matter. This results in Relational Leaders intentionally advancing their relationships while working on ways to apply Principle #4: Value People Before Processes. Through analysis and working with over two hundred clients, I have concluded that intentionally advancing 70 to 80 percent of your business relationships into this dimension leads to high-performing relationships and results.

Let's start by going back to Jason's second goal, which involves a very important project centered on integrating a new product from a joint venture that he is leading. If you have ever worked on a project of this nature you know there are many dynamics and activities to consider, such as product availability, product messaging and rollout, co-branding, sales education and web presence. However, the most important dynamic is usually the one that is most assumed or simply ignored—the relationships required to have a new revenue-producing product in the market. Therefore, in order to connect the important relationships to the new product integration, figure 9-2 illustrates Jason's goal and a key team member sponsor, José. You will notice that Jason needs to advance his existing relationship with José, a Boomer, with whom he has worked on prior projects. Jason strategically decides to advance his relationship with José to that of a Professional Peer as the best relationship strategy based on the scope and impact of his goal. Remember, Professional Peers are defined as an advanced business relationship around common goals where there is no perceived role/hierarchy when working together. In other words, Professional Peers are just two hardworking, well-intentioned professionals seeking to get stuff done. By the way, their role or level in the company does not impact their ability to get things done either.

Goal	IBR	Demographic	Colleague, Professional Peer, Advocate
Integrate new product from strategic alliance partner into pipeline by the end of the second quarter	José	Δ	Professional Peer

Figure 9-2. Jason's Business Relationship Assessment: Professional Peer.

In this scenario, Jason has multiple relationships that will ultimately determine the success of the project. However, the prioritization of relationships begins with José and then moves to the other team members. For this example, we will first focus on his relationship advancement with José because they each need a strong relationship to then support the level of relationship complexity that the team members face as they seek support outside of the team. I will address this after Jason works through his action planning for José.

Therefore, here's a two-phased approach for Jason with José and ultimately with José and the team to value people before processes:

1. Focus on advancing the relationship with José to that of a Professional Peer by establishing a personal value proposition for the relationship.
2. Understand and leverage the strength of relationships among the team members and across the company so the team can accomplish its goal.

CAPABILITY BUILDER

Before moving ahead with Jason, please record behaviors you have experienced when advancing successful business relationships with Professional Peers, based on your personal and professional experiences. What in your approach prompted these behaviors/responses?

Colleague Behavior	Approach

▶ *Focus on Advancing the Relationship with José*

Jason had previously developed a Colleague dimension business relationship with José and now needs to advance it based on what is in essence both of their goals around the integration of the new product from the alliance partner.

Value Propositions

What exactly is a value proposition? Experts from Kaplan and Norton of *The Balanced Scorecard* to marketing guru Michael Porter do a wonderful job of defining a company's value proposition. In general, after reviewing their extensive work, I concluded that a value proposition can be defined as follows: A clear statement, through the eyes of the other party, that provides some kind of benefit.

How do Relational Leaders adapt this thinking to their work? I am asked that question time and time again because I spend a great deal of time helping clients develop value propositions.

So how then can we translate that shorthand back to Jason in order for him to be effective in advancing his relationship with José to the Professional Peer dimension? Relational Leaders first develop a personal value proposition as a way to advance the relationship with their Colleagues to reach the Professional Peer dimension and to value people before processes. It is in essence Jason's personal value proposition as a leader in working with José to advance his relationship in pursuit of their common goal of integrating the new product offering from the alliance.

Jason's Personal Value Proposition

Since all of Jason's hard skills, product, industry knowledge and experiences are a given, they may not be distinguishing from a personal value proposition perspective. A personal value proposition is in essence a literal statement of how Jason personally brings value to the relationship and opportunity. Since José is likely working with many other people, how will the experience of collaborating with Jason make it exceptional?

Jason can follow these steps to develop his personal value proposition:

- Know José's GPS
- Know himself—what does he do particularly well as a leader?
- Make it personal to José

▶ Know José's GPS

Jason has worked with José previously and has captured his GPS in the Relational Agility Action Planner that follows. He should continue to explore and update this information so he can tailor his personal value proposition to José's GPS.

▶ *Know Himself*

Here's a worksheet (figure 9-3) for Jason to use to develop his sources of value for his relationship with José on this project:

	Source of Value	How Presented	Benefit to José
1	Launched new product with alliance partner	Summary of successes and challenges with this project	Jason's history with the project should make it less risky for José to support his decisions
2	Knows from José's GPS that he is looking to retire in a few years	Acknowledge that he has prioritized this due to José's succession planning	Helps José balance between working and planning to retire
3			
4			
5			

Figure 9-3. Jason's sources of value worksheet.

CAPABILITY BUILDER

Using the following template (figure 9-4), record your sources of value that people recognize when working with you.

	Source of Value	How Presented	Benefit
1			
2			
3			
4			
5			

Figure 9-4. Sources of value template.

▶ *Make It Personal with José*

Jason takes the input and thinking from sources 1 and 2 and develops the following personal value proposition: When working with me, José can expect the team to deliver on its commitments within the budget and with a minimum of surprises, based on my track record of leadership around these projects.

This statement is clear, connects with a goal of José's and then adds an element of personalization with Jason. Jason may never actually need to state this personal value proposition because he has a track record as a Colleague with José where he previously built Relational Capital. Therefore, if done well and delivered upon, Jason's personal value proposition should just emerge. However, if necessary, Jason can share a personal story about working with José or another group to reinforce this ability to deliver on his leadership.

For example, during an interaction with José, Jason can share: "José, remember that joint venture project a few years back that was considered a huge success? I recall that we took the approach of focusing on the types of people involved, where relationships existed and any gaps that needed to be filled prior to any process design. This was the major contributing factor to our success."

In fact, Jason as a Relational Leader is a living and breathing value proposition, so here is his Relational Agility Action Planner for José that now includes a personal value proposition (figure 9-5):

IBR	Role	
José	Director of Project Management	
Desired Relationship Status		
☐ Colleague	☑ Professional Peer	☐ Advocate
Goal Connecting Me with IBR?	**What Is My Relationship Strategy?**	
Integrate new product from strategic alliance partner into pipeline at the end of the second quarter	Advance to Professional Peer dimension through delivering on personal value proposition from previous interactions; work with José to ensure team's relationships are aligned prior to process design	
Goals	**Passions**	**Struggles**
Ensure his functional team is in good shape prior to retiring in a few years	Loves fly-fishing with his family	Management considering downsizing his functional group
Key Points (Reminders for Jason)		
José is a Boomer; facing pre-retirement challenges; FIND WAYS TO MAKE THIS PROJECT EASIER FOR JOSÉ DUE TO HIS COMMITMENT TO HIS TEAM AND STRUGGLES Deliver on personal value proposition: *When working with me, José can expect the team to deliver on its commitments within the budget and with a minimum of surprises, based on my track record of leadership around these projects.*		

Figure 9-5. Jason's Relational Agility Action Planner for José.

Jason's action plan for his relationship with José evolves to a higher level of significance based on the team's goal and the level of relationship that Jason determines that he needs to advance with José. The inclusion of his personal value proposition is noteworthy as well.

LATERAL AND VERTICAL RELATIONSHIP PLANNING

Now that Jason and José are aligned and their relationship is advancing into the Professional Peer dimension, the next step to actualize Principle #4: Value People Before Processes involves factoring in the relationships of the other members within the team and across the company so they can accomplish the team's goal of integrating the new product from their alliance partner. Lateral and Vertical Relationship Planning is an approach that is all about how Relational Leaders are intentional about human beings during the process development phase of planning. Remember the cable company example where process was valued before people?

Thinking Between the Boxes

Lateral and Vertical Relationship Planning is an intentional, practical way to determine if Jason and José are "thinking between the boxes" during process design and where the relational gaps exist that will create real challenges for the project. If we reflect on the various organizational charts and models that I shared earlier in this book, the assumption is that relationships exist already—the solid lines. If the team members simply think outside the box, as many management gurus recommend, they will miss critical relational gaps between the process boxes. It is far better to identify these up front prior to any process design that could end up subverting their common goal of integrating the new product from their alliance partner. Figure 9-6 is a way to visualize where to locate these lateral and vertical relationships.

Figure 9-6. Lateral and vertical relationships.

The following steps and table help team members record their important business relationships needed to support the project:

1. Identify existing team member IBRs (boss, peers, team members) who could be helpful to the project; determine dimension and generation

2. Identify the At-Will important business relationship connections (boss, peers, team members) where relationships may be needed; determine dimension and generation

3. Record results from steps 1 and 2 in the table in figure 9-7:

IBR	Last Meeting	Next Meeting	Relationship Status	Generation
Warren—Finance	Today	In 1 week	Professional Peer	Δ
Pete—IT			At-Will Colleague	≈
Mae—Marketing			At-Will Colleague	#
Diane—Customer Service	2 months ago	Pending	At-Will Professional Peer	#
Jeff—Operations	1 year ago		Colleague	Δ

Figure 9-7. Relationship complexity.

Lateral and Vertical Relationship Requirements

You'll notice that step 2 allows Jason and the team to expand the table for the next level of relationship beyond their most proximate important business relationships that they need to launch and advance in pursuit of the project goal. These lateral and vertical relationships are complex because some relationships exist and others are at-will. There is a strong chance that the people the team connects with have no knowledge of the team's need, let alone have factored these into their own performance goals for the year. So now you have a team heading into the enterprise firing off "synapses" to accomplish their objectives without any real strategy for the relationships needed to accomplish them. This very simple assessment provides a lens into the relational risk inherent in the project not just within the team but across the enterprise. The chart in figure 9-7 is an example of the relationship complexity I shared in chapter 1 and reveals where the team needs to focus its relational efforts. The above result is typical in that a few dates and some information are filled in, but the majority of the table is filled with white space indicating no initial or ongoing contact with the other IBRs. Here's where Principle #4 comes into play. The more white space relationally, the increase in risk to the project due to the lack of even minor relationship connections or synapses during process development. This results in process taking over in deference to the relationships with the people. How can Jason and the team members overcome this relational challenge and inherent risk to the project? In order to "think between the boxes" of process planning, the team's goal is to ensure that all of the boxes are filled in so the process design will increase the project's chance for success. Then the team should consider the next ongoing steps to debrief and continue to refresh their intentional relationship thinking:

4. Discuss with the full team and create Relational Agility action plans for IBRs

5. Review IBR status during team meetings

6. Adjust relational strategy as needed

For steps 4 through 6, discuss results of the previous steps with the team and create action plans for the IBRs identified as the key to success of the projects, then review progress as a team and make adjustments as necessary. Figure 9-8 is an example of a template to summarize this important information so that it can be processed on an ongoing basis when the team comes together to assess where it stands relationally.

Contact Name	Position	Goals, Role & Responsibilities	Goal for Relationship	Action Items

Figure 9-8. Team relationship gap analysis template.

CAPABILITY BUILDER

Review the following questions that a team should discuss when developing relationship strategies and select the questions most applicable to the project you are currently working on:

❑ Which of our colleagues do we need to connect with who can directly support this project?

❑ Who do we need to connect with who indirectly could create influence for the project?

❑ Where do we stand relationally with each of the above?

❑ What level are the relationships today?

❑ What relational strategies do we need to develop?

INTRODUCTIONS MATTER

Before closing this chapter, I want to share my belief that introductions matter regardless of whether they are outside or within a company. Relational Leaders who work with customers are generally very aware that a referral or introduction by an important customer relationship is the most powerful way to profitably grow their business. High-performing Relational Leaders make seeking referrals part of their regular work flow. However, as I just demonstrated, Relational Leaders are continually faced with At-Will relationships that require the same amount of care as new customer relationships. Relational Leaders who understand this and then foster strong relationships are able to move projects and activities along much better when they:

- Understand that their Professional Peer and Advocate relationships are a great source of introductions within the organization
- Develop strategies as part of their action planning to accomplish their objectives through targeted introductions as much as possible

CAPABILITY BUILDER

Reflect on a recent completed project or initiative. How did introductions impact the results? How would other introductions have impacted the results?

_____

_____

Now that Jason has launched his Colleague relationship with Ashley and advanced his relationship to the Professional Peer dimension with José while moving the team's relationships forward laterally and vertically, he now can move into the rare air of elevating to an Advocate-level relationship with Beth in chapter 10.

Relational Leaders are the value proposition!

10

ELEVATING RELATIONSHIPS WITH ADVOCATES

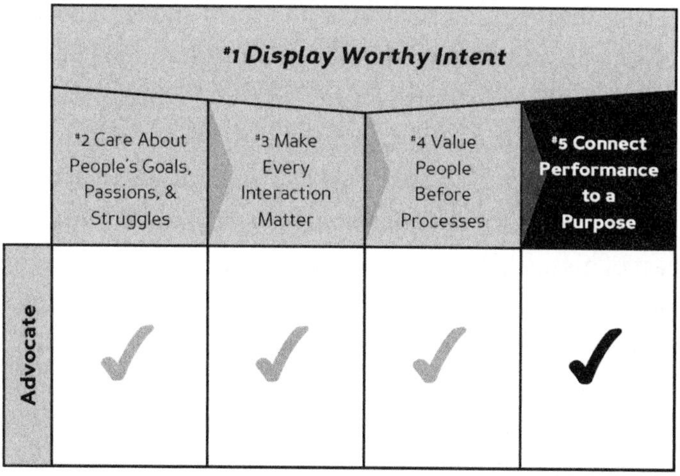

#1 Display Worthy Intent			
#2 Care About People's Goals, Passions, & Struggles	#3 Make Every Interaction Matter	#4 Value People Before Processes	**#5 Connect Performance to a Purpose**
✓	✓	✓	✓

Figure 10-1. Relational Agility Process: Advocate.

THIS CHAPTER IS ABOUT how Relational Leaders amplify their Relational Agility to elevate relationships to the Advocate dimension. The Relational Agility Process will illustrate that collaborators can strategize and become intentional around the Five Principles by emphasizing the relevant principles as needed.

Elevating is "additive" from Colleague and Professional Peer dimensions. The Relational Leader builds off the Relational Capital invested and how it allows her to take things to the highest level by focusing on connecting performance to a real purpose. In a perfect world, we would want everyone to be Advocates, but as I mentioned previously we only have so much time to invest in specific relationships to accomplish common goals. Again the need to elevate to an Advocate level is born out of goals and needs and sometimes there is immediacy to take a relationship to this dimension.

NOW JASON NEEDS AN ADVOCATE

Let's continue by going back to Jason's third and final goal, which involves a $1 million unbudgeted investment for one of his projects. Figure 10-2 illustrates Jason's goal and his sponsor, Beth, a Gen with whom he has worked many times before. Jason has strategically decided to advance his relationship with Beth to that of an Advocate as the best relationship strategy based on the scope and impact of his goal. Remember Advocates have career-spanning relationships that go beyond the scope of the common goals the Relational Leaders have worked on previously.

Goal	IBR	Demographic	Colleague, Professional Peer, Advocate
Seek executive committee approval for unbudgeted $1 million investment	Beth	≈	Advocate

Figure 10-2. Jason's Business Relationship Assessment: Advocate.

Because Jason has built up Relational Capital with Beth over many interactions and years, he can "pass go" immediately by developing his action plan with a focus on collaborating with Beth directly to accomplish this goal (figure 10-3).

IBR	Role
Beth	Executive/Board Member

Desired Relationship Status

☐ Colleague	☐ Professional Peer	☑ Advocate

Goal Connecting Me with IBR?	What Is My Relationship Strategy?	
Seek executive committee approval for unbudgeted $1 million investment	Elevate to Advocate dimension by working with Beth to develop a project-level value proposition that connects the investment to a meaningful purpose	

Goals	Passions	Struggles
Become high-performing member of the board	Spending time with her kids; writing a book on women's leadership	Pending divorce creating emotional and capacity challenges at work

Key Points (Reminders for Jason)

Beth is a Gen; hard-driving professional facing personal challenges at home; FIND WAYS TO SUPPORT AND HELP BALANCE BETH'S DIVERSE GPS

Personal value proposition: *When working with me, Beth can expect our interactions to be focused on the highest level contributions we can make and how the work makes a meaningful difference*

Figure 10-3. Jason's Relational Agility Action Planner for Beth.

CAPABILITY BUILDER

Based on your personal and professional goals and experiences, identify you own "Beths" who you need to elevate your business relationship to an Advocate dimension with:

1. _____

2. _____

3. _____

PROJECT VALUE PROPOSITION

Since his business relationship with Beth is already in the Professional Peer dimension, Jason had previously created a personal value proposition as per his action plan in figure 10-3. And now that he has created his action plan to elevate his relationship with Beth, he needs to focus on how to align their work with Principle #5: Connect Performance to a Purpose. I shared the idea of a personal value proposition in chapter 9 for Jason's individual work with José and in getting the team aligned around their integration goal. Working with Beth to come up with a project value proposition will help develop higher level rationale for the unbudgeted investment and should help support elevating their mutual relationship to the Advocate dimension.

Look at Jason and Beth's common goal: *Seek executive committee approval for unbudgeted $1 million investment.* They should ask themselves the following:

- What is the reason the money is needed?
- How did this come about?
- Why would the board consider it?
- Who else do they need to build relationships with to create additional support?
- Where do they stand relationally with those others?
- What rationale can be used to create real meaning for the request?

Let's assume that the project where the unbudgeted funds are needed is for a new HR system and that Jason and Beth work through the questions as follows:

- What is the reason the money is needed?
  - Additional features required that were not originally scoped

- How did this come about?
  - The acquisition of a foreign company happened quickly that was not planned during the scoping of the system
- Why would the board consider it?
  - Otherwise two separate HR systems will be needed to ensure legal compliance and employee support leading to inconsistency and the chance for missteps with human capital
- Who else do they need to build relationships with and where do they stand relationally?
  - Identified the following: CFO, VP of HR, chairman of the board
- What rationale can be used to create real meaning for the request?
  - Acquisitions typically fail to meet objectives because the people are the last thing considered beyond benefits and payroll
  - Cultural and operational risks will be developed further and used to support the request on an ROI basis

CAPABILITY BUILDER

Write a project value proposition that connects performance to a purpose for Jason and Beth's goal and then compare with the example that follows:

_____

_____

Project Value Proposition Example for Jason and Beth's Goal of Securing $1 Million in Unbudgeted Funds for New HRM Project

By approving this investment for additional HRM functionality, our ability to focus on the new employees' needs will be increased while the performance of the new acquisition will result in an ROI of 2.5 times the investment required.

RECEPTIVE WILL AND OVERCOMING DISTRACTORS

The Relational Agility Process is all about powerful collaborations that must be driven by strong, mutual relationships. When I think about mutual relationships, the term "Receptive Will" comes to mind. I like to use this term to describe the quality or attribute needed by Relational Leaders when they work together. If business relationships are going to break down corporate silos, navigate the complexity that I shared in chapter 1, cross generational gaps and create great business performance, then when humans collaborate they need to have a Receptive Will—*the attribute of being open to another person's outreach and nonjudgmental around the purpose for that outreach.* Sounds pretty simple, right? However, people are in fact human and challenged by many factors that may prevent this attribute from emerging. While I strived to make this a very positive book and experience for my readers, I am also realistic and as we all know in business and life there are those who do not display Worthy Intent toward us. This could delay or damage our potential to reach our highest level of development. I call these distractors and while many technological culprits exist, let's focus on my top five human distractors:

1. **Happy Hank**—always available to talk about the game over the weekend; hangs out in your work area making small talk; takes credit when things go well; disappears when challenges emerge

2. **Negative Nellie**—always something negative to say about the project or company; blames others for their issues; fails to acknowledge others

3. **Demeaning Doug**—talks down to everyone; always looking for cover when challenges occur

4. **Emailing Edwina**—copies everyone and their brother on emails, in effect taking time away from everyone; always looking to cover themselves

5. **Meeting Marvin**—calls meetings for even the simplest things; takes endless notes; expects everyone to read them to the nth degree

In practical terms, these are roadblocks of negative energy that bring you and your relationships down. Colleague and Professional Peer dimensions can be impacted by these more than Advocate dimension relationships because Advocates create an immunity due to the long-term Relational Capital invested in them. Advocates deal with roadblocks seamlessly, while Professional Peers and Colleagues need to increase Relational Capital to overcome these challenges.

SO WHAT'S A RELATIONAL LEADER TO DO?

Throughout this book I established that Relational Leaders *intentionally* align with and utilize the Five Principles upon which this book is based to launch, advance and elevate their important business relationships. Relational Leaders can overcome distractors through that same ability and display Worthy Intent as follows:

- Connecting the need to collaborate around common goals with distractors
- Asking questions to understand and care about the goals, passions and struggles of the distractor

- Demonstrating to the distractor that every interaction matters by:
  - Balancing small talk
  - Listening and not judging negatively
  - Addressing challenges
  - Modeling email etiquette
  - Planning and scheduling effective meetings that end early

Relational Leaders use their Receptive Will along with the above approach that is aligned with the first three principles (display Worthy Intent; care about people's goals, passions and struggles; and make every interaction matter) when they attempt to overcome distractors. Hopefully, in most cases, they will be successful. But we all know and have experienced the distractor who is not willing to return that same Receptive Will, despite our best intentions. In this case, and I truly believe in this approach, the Relational Leader more or less needs to find a way to "punt" the business relationship because the business relationship and performance processes are being compromised. Companies have many protocols to deal with challenging employees and while I am not advocating "telling on" your Negative Nellie, I am encouraging Relational Leaders to avoid adapting to the style of the distractor by providing direct feedback during the process as to why you believe the relationship and performance are struggling. If attempts to overcome distractors through the principles and feedback conversations are not working, then bringing in an objective leader to arbitrate the issue is the only option left. During that process the Relational Leader needs to ask out of the business relationship and seek a new Colleague to work with on the common goal. Now that we are through with overcoming distractors, let's move on to more appealing work.

RELATIONAL AGILITY PROCESS SUMMARY

The Relational Agility Process in figure 10-4 displays the complete approach for Relational Leaders to harness the power of Worthy Intent around their goals and business relationships. I mentioned earlier that Relational Leaders do not have time to take everyone to the Advocate dimension. True Relational Agility is when the Relational Leader consciously determines based on her goals what dimension will be required relationally to accomplish them while ensuring alignment with Worthy Intent. You will notice that the how-to concepts and steps to achieve each dimension are included in the Relational Agility Process. Also I hear from business professionals all the time, "How many relationships should I have in each dimension to be successful?" Of course, my answer is always, "It depends on your goals and the time you have." Through my research and analysis of over twenty-five thousand relationships generated by over five thousand professionals, I have come up with a persona rule for where a Relational Leader's relationships should fall into the Relational Agility Process:

Business Relationship Dimension Breakout
- **15 percent Colleagues**—should always have new relationships entering the Relational Agility Process as well as relationships that are most effective remaining in this dimension
- **75–80 percent Professional Peers**—this is the sweet spot in the process because Relational Leaders work most effectively here and there are many opportunities for elevating to the Advocate dimension
- **5–10 percent Advocates**—career-spanning, apex relationships that require ongoing Relational Capital investment

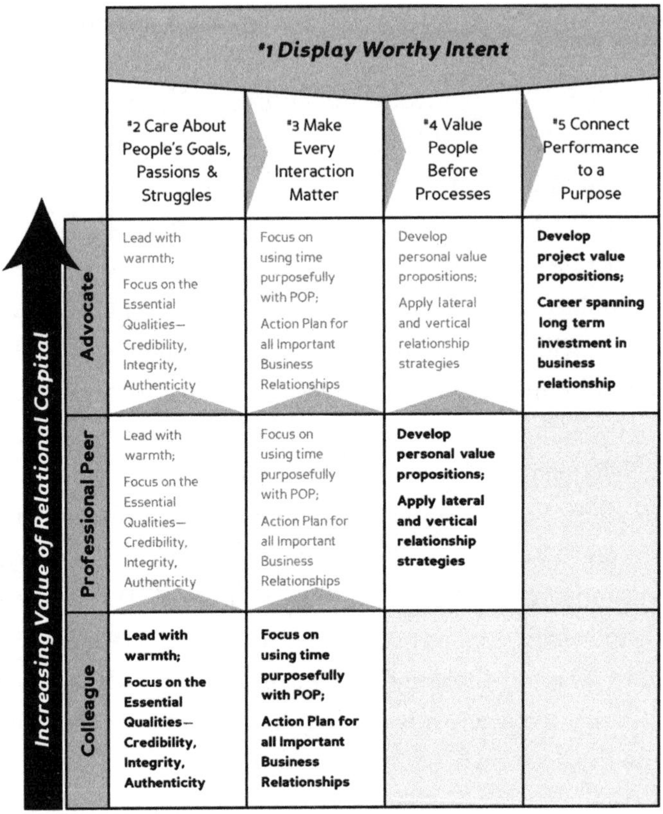

*1 Display Worthy Intent			
*2 Care About People's Goals, Passions & Struggles	***3 Make Every Interaction Matter**	***4 Value People Before Processes**	***5 Connect Performance to a Purpose**
Advocate — Lead with warmth; Focus on the Essential Qualities— Credibility, Integrity, Authenticity	Focus on using time purposefully with POP; Action Plan for all Important Business Relationships	Develop personal value propositions; Apply lateral and vertical relationship strategies	**Develop project value propositions; Career spanning long term investment in business relationship**
Professional Peer — Lead with warmth; Focus on the Essential Qualities— Credibility, Integrity, Authenticity	Focus on using time purposefully with POP; Action Plan for all Important Business Relationships	**Develop personal value propositions; Apply lateral and vertical relationship strategies**	
Colleague — **Lead with warmth; Focus on the Essential Qualities— Credibility, Integrity, Authenticity**	**Focus on using time purposefully with POP; Action Plan for all Important Business Relationships**		

Increasing Value of Relational Capital

Figure 10-4. Relational Agility Process.

Congratulations, you have completed Parts I and II of *The Relationship Engine*! Now let's explore putting it all together in Part III: "Becoming a Relational Leader: A Practical Approach" so you can complete your Relational Leadership journey and begin connecting with the people who power your business.

Relational Leaders create career-spanning business relationships with Advocates.

PART II EXECUTIVE SUMMARY

The Relational Agility Process was developed in great detail throughout Part II. Here's a refresher for you to refer back to after you complete this book and continue on your journey to Relational Leadership.

Relational Leader Insights

- Relational Agility is the Relational Leader's capability to apply the Five Principles to collaborate effectively with Colleagues, Professional Peers and Advocates leading to superior performance
- Relational Agility Process is a process that Relational Leaders use to harness the power of Worthy Intent so they fluidly conduct collaborative interactions regardless of role, status or generation
- Dimensionality is the categorization of At-Will business relationships as Colleague, Professional Peers and Advocates
- The four steps of Intentionality
  - Determine your goals.
  - Attach your goals to real people by relationship dimension.
  - Develop strategies for each relationship.
  - Implement by using the Relational Agility Process for launching, advancing or elevating your IBRs.
- Launching relationships with Colleagues is all about a warmth approach seeking to uncover Relational GPS and to make every interaction matter by bringing in the qualities of Credibility, Integrity and Authenticity.
- Relational Leaders plan their meetings effectively using

the POP approach; they call their meetings at times that are convenient for all participants.

- Action planning for your important business relationships is a proactive way to launch your Colleague relationships and allows for advancing and elevating relationships in the future.

- Relational Leaders apply Principle #4: Value People Before Processes by focusing on the relationships needed to accomplish goals prior to process design.

- A value proposition is a *clear statement, through the eyes of the other party, that provides some kind of benefit.*

- Referrals and introductions are just as important within a company as outside.

- Relational Leaders make a conscious decision to elevate relationships to an Advocate dimension.

- The need to elevate to an Advocate dimension is born out of common goals between Relational Leaders and the desire to take them to a higher purpose.

- Receptive Will is the attribute of being open to another person's outreach and nonjudgmental around the purpose for that outreach.

ULTIMATE CAPABILITY BUILDER

Review your company mission and how it makes a difference in the world. Then using that insight as guidance, create a value proposition for a key project you are working on to align it with Principle #5: Connect Performance to a Purpose:

_____

_____

PART III

BECOMING A RELATIONAL LEADER: A PRACTICAL APPROACH

11

TOOLS FOR THE RELATIONAL LEADER

THERE IS AN OLD saying in sports that you do not win games on paper, meaning that the team with the better statistics and perceived superior athletes does not always translate to winning. When it comes to Relationship Intentionality, I believe that Relational Leaders do win on paper because a significant piece of Intentionality is to create plans and strategies like I've shared throughout this book. Therefore, this chapter provides you with the opportunity to apply some of the key tools that Relational Leaders intentionally use to launch, advance and elevate their most important business relationships. Each tool can stand on its own or be used systemically by you, an aspiring Relational Leader, in your quest to create exceptional experiences for other human beings.

MEASURING YOUR RELATIONSHIP STRENGTH

In chapter 1, when I asked, "Why do so few leaders say they actually do anything intentional or systematic toward developing relationships?" one common response was, "Relationships cannot be measured." But is that true? I sought out Dr. David Bush, the chairman of Villanova University's Masters in Human Resources program, to figure out an approach to measuring business relationships that anyone could use regardless of role, title, nationality and generation. We discussed the idea that the "assessment" should not involve psychology but be a reflection of the behaviors that aspiring Relational Leaders are observing.

I came up with thirty-five common behaviors that human beings exhibit when working together, and David validated that they were on target. We then tested, weighted, retested and continued to evolve the RQ Assessment to where it is today—an easy-to-use, immediately actionable way to measure your most important business relationships. With over twenty-five thousand relationships assessed to date and counting, RQ is the most used relationship assessment available and a mainstream way to align your goals with the most important business relationships you will need to launch, advance or elevate in order to accomplish them.

So to help you get started winning on paper, please use the following table to record your goals for the next six months and connect a person who you need to launch, advance or elevate a business relationship with to support you in accomplishing that specific goal:

My Goals	Important Business Relationship

Now that you have prioritized your business relationships with your goals, I would like to offer you the opportunity to take a complimentary RQ Assessment. While this assessment takes only about fifteen minutes to complete, the resulting analysis and suggestions will have an ongoing impact on your ability to achieve the strategies in your ensuing Relational Agility action plans in pursuit of your business goals.

Here's the link to create your free account and instructions for calculating your RQ that will allow you to create the foundation for your Relational Agility action plan: www.relationalcapitalgroup. com/tools/signup. If you have any questions or need any help, please contact us at info@relcapgroup.com.

The RQ Assessment will prompt you to answer five questions related to the thirty-five common behaviors that I mentioned earlier for each important business relationship. After you have answered the questions in the assessment as accurately and authentically as possible, you will be asked to click a button to calculate your RQ. This will generate your personalized RQ Summary, which will offer you:

- Your RQ score and range (the high and low potential of the specific relationships you assessed)
- The dimensional distribution of your relationships among Colleagues, Professional Peers and Advocates
- The level within each dimension
- Detailed suggestions on how to improve each of your business relationships
- Action plan templates to develop strategies for each business relationship

Once you have completed the RQ Assessment, please select *one* of the relationships you assessed and continue with the Relational Agility Action Planner that follows. Please be ready to record that relationship in the planner.

Relational Agility Action Planner

Throughout chapters 8 through 10, Jason worked to launch a relationship with a Colleague, advance multiple relationships with Professional Peers and elevate a relationship with a Professional Peer to that of an Advocate. The Relational Agility Action Planner used in each scenario represents an intentional and efficient way to plan for Jason's most important business relationships connected to his real goals. Here's the step-by-step instructions for you to take the relationship you selected from your RQ to complete your own Relational Agility action plan:

1. Record your important business relationship (IBR) and his role.
2. Decide which dimension will be required for this relationship.
3. Record the business goal attached to your IBR.
4. Develop a strategy for the IBR (continues to evolve).

5. Locate Relational GPS (continues to evolve).
6. Summarize key points—determine generation and develop personal value proposition using worksheet in figure 11-1.
7. Review and upgrade Relational Agility action plan as needed.

IBR	Role

Desired Relationship Status		
❑ Colleague	❑ Professional Peer	❑ Advocate

Goal Connecting Me with IBR?	What Is My Relationship Strategy?	

Goals	Passions	Struggles

Key Points

IBR's generation

❑ Λ Boomers

❑ ≈ Gens

❑ # Millennials

Personal Value Proposition Worksheet

1. Know your Colleague's GPS (see above)
2. Know yourself (see the sources of value template, figure 9-4)
3. Make it personal (use a personal story to demonstrate your personal value proposition)
Commitment to Deliver Personal Value Proposition:
I will communicate and deliver on this personal value proposition by this date: ___ /___ /_____
NOTES:

Figure 11-1. Relational Agility Action Planner.

Lateral and Vertical Relationship Templates

In chapter 9, I shared the need for Relational Leaders to think beyond their immediate important business relationships and think laterally and vertically to ensure that their goals are being supported among the many At-Will relationships required. Here are two tools that will help you and your team intentionally think beyond the important business relationship that you just assessed in RQ and action planned for in support of your goals.

Lateral and Vertical Relationships

Based on the important business relationship you assessed, please record at least one lateral relationship and one vertical relationship in the lines provided:

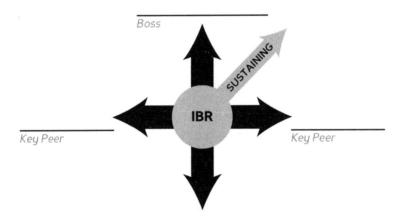

Figure 11-2. Lateral and vertical relationship exercise.

Lateral and Vertical Gap Analysis

Complete the lateral and vertical gap analysis template (figure 11-3) to determine how much white space exists laterally and vertically with the relationships you selected above and develop plans to get these next-level important business relationships moving in pursuit of your goals.

IBR	Last Meeting	Next Meeting	Relationship Status (Colleague, Professional Peer, Advocate)	Generation (Boomer, Gen, Millennial)

Figure 11-3. Lateral and vertical relationship gap analysis template.

TOP TEN OBSERVABLE BEHAVIORS FOR RELATIONAL LEADERS

I shared in chapter 2 that Relational Leaders are strong observers of human behavior. Here's a checklist of key behaviors that Relational Leaders should experience as they launch, advance and elevate their business relationships. Please use this checklist to gauge your relational progress with your important business relationship.

Please consider your IBR from your Relational Agility Action Planner in this chapter and check as many boxes that apply:

- ❏ Your Worthy Intent is validated through the words and actions of others.
- ❏ Goals, Passions and Struggles are readily shared with you.
- ❏ Confidences are shared.
- ❏ Meeting times are extended to process your ideas and needs.

❏ You benefit from unsolicited introductions and referrals.

❏ You are included in strategic thinking and planning.

❏ Executives seek you out to join key initiatives.

❏ Your opinion matters when connecting performance to a purpose.

❏ You are included in key social events.

❏ Your relationships are fun.

Depending on where you stand relationally—Colleague, Professional Peer or Advocate—you will have from zero to ten boxes checked off. Here's a scoring insight that serves as a rule of thumb:

❏ Colleague: 0–4

❏ Professional Peer: 5–7

❏ Advocate: 8–10

Please remember that strategies for achieving Colleague, Professional Peer and Advocate dimension relationships are relative based on your goals. The key takeaway is that you should make sure your relationship strategy is aligned with your goals before going through the checklist. If your responses come back with a Colleague score and you need an Advocate relationship, then more Relational Capital investment and time are required.

CONDUCTING IMPACTFUL MEETINGS

Relational Leaders value the time of their important business relationships and model this through their effective leadership of meetings. I introduced the POP (purpose, outcomes, process) approach in chapter 8 as a way to make meetings feel more like a great investment of time rather than a cost to the participants. Here is an exercise to help you prepare for your next meeting with the important business relationship you identified and are working with in this chapter using a well-designed POP.

- Develop a POP for a future meeting you are planning to hold.
- For the purpose statement, answer the following questions based on the perceived benefits of the meeting:
  - What am I trying to accomplish?
  - Why will the participants benefit?
  - Do I have the right participants?
  - How much time do I need?
  - Do I even need to call this meeting?
- Outcomes: What value and next steps will the participants leave with?
- Process: How will we get to the purpose and outcomes?

POP Template

Purpose Statement ("what" are we trying to do and "why"?)
- To

_____

- So that

_____

Outcomes (Results/Takeaways)

1. _____
2. _____
3. _____

Process

- Introduce specific meeting topic (topic leader)
- Dialogue on topic (group)
- Capture any agreements and/or commitments on the topic (note taker)
- Introduce next meeting topic—open items to close process (team member)
- Repeat dialogue and capture steps above
- Arrive at a path forward (meeting leader)
- Close meeting within promised time period (meeting leader)
- Document team agreements and participant commitments and launch next meeting with an update on these for continuity

Relational Leaders develop personal value propositions for important business relationships. Personal value propositions begin with the Relational Leader recording their sources of value and corresponding benefits. Please complete the table in figure 11-4 for the sources of value you bring to your important business relationships:

	Source of Value	How Presented	Benefit
1			
2			
3			
4			
5			

Figure 11-4. Sources of value template

THE PERSONAL NATURE OF PENMANSHIP (HANDWRITTEN NOTES)

Relational Leaders create competitor-proof experiences for their colleagues whether they are internal or external to their companies. As I've mentioned many times during this book, their success comes through the experience they create for others. One surefire way to add to the experience is to personalize your thoughts using an actual pen and paper. Everyone uses email or text or some other electronic method to communicate today, including their notes of thanks. Those notes of thanks look like everyone else's on your colleagues' computer screens. Contrast that with the latest research that indicates the typical business professional receives handwritten mail or notes less than 1 percent of the time. Relational Leaders stand out and distinguish themselves through the power of writing handwritten notes. Personalized, handwritten notes provide a sense of thoughtfulness to the receiver unlike anything electronically generated based on the following:

- Your personalized handwritten note will likely be the only one your colleague receives that entire month or longer
- Colleagues will physically interact with your note through opening the envelope and handling it versus reading lines on a screen
- Demonstrates you cared about your interaction based on your comments and summary of next steps
- The act of writing with a pen alone requires and demonstrates additional care and connotes how the relationship is valued
- Leaves the recipient with the sense that working with you will be a distinctive experience

Three Rules of Thumb for Personalized Handwritten Notes
1. Use only after meaningful initial interactions and/or to acknowledge significant milestones.
2. Keep your notes brief and to the point, recalling specifics so you can tailor your message.
3. Carefully pen your notes so the recipient can understand your thoughts; sign off with your own distinctive message, such as "best to you," "kind regards," etc.

Sample follow-up note:

> Hi, Laura.
>
> It was a pleasure meeting you and learning about the new enterprise project. I will send along the draft designs to you later this week. Looking forward to our next interaction.
>
> Best to you,
>
> Ed

Draft a handwritten note to your important business relationship highlighting an important aspect of your latest interaction and proposed next steps.

_____

_____

_____

Relational Leadership begins by winning on paper!

12

TAKE THE RELATIONAL LEADER CHALLENGE

NOW IT'S TIME TO challenge yourself and discover your level of fluency with *The Relationship Engine*. I have shared principles, concepts, qualities, processes, anecdotes, nomenclature and tools throughout this book. This chapter presents a series of five short essays about real Relational Leaders followed by a checklist of the top ten attributes that may apply to their relational approach. There are five correct answers for each essay. A perfect score of 25 would indicate that you have done a superior job of internalizing the concepts from this book and their application in each essay.

HINT: Two of the five answers are exactly the same for each essay. These two responses are aligned with *The Relationship Engine*'s central message and are foundational for important business relationships. The five correct responses for each essay are displayed below each essay's scorecard. Have fun and good luck!

1. LYLE'S RELATIONAL LEADERSHIP

Lyle is the general manager of a pharmaceutical manufacturing and development company that makes more than 90 million units per year and is working on getting forty or fifty new products to market each year. Lyle has responsibility for more than eight hundred company employees. But when he looks at his role and the decisions he makes, he thinks beyond the eight hundred employees to their families (spouses, children, extended family) and estimates as many as three thousand people could be impacted. He realizes that since the company is not located in an area like the Northeast United States, where manufacturing jobs are plentiful, poor executive decisions can really cause some damage to his employees. He likes to say, "My hope is that our families can count on us," acknowledging they have mortgages, car payments, healthcare concerns and tuition payments just like "most folks." Lyle notes how some employees have been working at his company for over ten years after their mom or dad worked there for twenty or more years. He realizes that these "folks" need to know there is predictability and stability when they come to work every day. We discussed some distractors to Relational Leaders in chapter 10, and here are some potential distractors that Lyle aims to avoid:

1. Safety concerns
2. Job instability
3. Lack of communication leading to speculation
4. No visibility to the top
5. Job market

The Impact of Town Hall Meetings

Twice every year he meets with all employees below the supervisor level (about 550 people) who work with him and his management team. Lyle visits their locations and talks with everyone from maintenance workers to scientists in what he calls "town hall meetings." None of his management team is there so that employees are less concerned about what their bosses might think. Lyle first addresses company-wide, big-picture initiatives before opening the floor for general inquiries. While he cannot process everything during the town hall meeting, his assistant creates a list of topics to bring back to Lyle's team for additional analysis and thinking.

Every session yields some worthwhile talking points that would have eventually made their way to Lyle like "four-times filtered coffee," in his words, had he not gone to the grassroots level. Lyle stresses that this is not a negative toward his management team; they are extremely dedicated to the values he espouses, but they are also extremely busy just keeping the plants running, so issues may not be able to move forward as fast unless they get to Lyle directly. For example, employees at one plant complained the HVAC system wouldn't run at night, making the overnight shift uncomfortably warm in the summertime. It kept coming up at the plant level and the plant manager looked into it, but he could not figure it out despite a great deal of effort. Somehow the AC was hardwired in a way that it would not run overnight. Plant managers have a great deal to do, so the problem was stuck in neutral. When this came up in a town hall meeting, Lyle was able to get a better understanding of it and had their HVAC vendor troubleshoot the issue. They found the "ghost" hardwire and now the plant has air conditioning around the clock.

The town hall approach really pays off from a performance standpoint. Lyle is convinced that this connection to his employees at the grassroots level has led to the following performance improvements:

- Consistently higher profit and labor utilization
- Increased on-time service approaching 97 percent

- Reduction in error rates
- Low turnover in specialized skilled areas
- And most importantly, happy employees!

Relational Leader Concept	Identified
1. Worthy Intent	
2. Care About People's GPS	
3. Make Every Interaction Matter	
4. Value People Before Processes	
5. Connect Performance to a Purpose	
6. Intentionality	
7. Credibility	
8. Integrity	
9. Authenticity	
10. Business Performance	
Total Correct Answers	

Correct Responses: 1, 2, 5, 8, 10

2. THE BARKANN FAMILY HEALING HEARTS FOUNDATION

If you've ever watched Comcast SportsNet in Philadelphia, there's a very good chance you have seen sports anchor Michael Barkann talking about the typically woeful state of Philly sports. What you might not realize is that Michael along with his wife, Ellen, started a charity called the Barkann Family Healing Hearts Foundation. The remarkable thing about this charity is that it doesn't operate through a higher institution, like a hospital, for example. The Healing Hearts Foundation is for families who need help in a pinch—those who need immediate financial assistance when a loved one falls ill, or worse. The charity skips bureaucratic processes and gives financial aid right away. Ellen likes to say, "We help bridge the gap for people in desperate need."

While the foundation has many incredible Relational Leaders, for the purpose of this essay, Ellen and Michael suggested that I highlight the Barkann Family Healing Hearts Foundation's executive director, Mike Barnes, and how he has almost single-handedly grown the foundation's outreach and network. From a background perspective, Mike has dealt with more personal obstacles that anyone should have in their lifetime, so he could be easily excused if he were cold or unfriendly. Yet, when you talk with Mike, you might find yourself asking, "How could anyone be that nice and authentic?" It's a question the Barkanns themselves asked after first meeting Mike. However, over time, his performance spoke for itself and it was clear Mike was creating lasting relationships and had been for some time. Forty percent of the supporters that helped the foundation were friends of Mike, and 20 percent were actually Mike's high school classmates.

Perhaps the most striking aspect of Mike's Relational Leadership is the fact that a number of families who received help from the foundation later came back to help *other* families. Mike goes beyond basic At-Will relationships and creates lifelong bonds, which end up serving him and the Healing Hearts Foundation long after initial contact. He's the type of guy who overdelivers on commitments and whose spirit is contagious. The results, especially in the case of the Healing Hearts Foundation, are life-changing. Since Mike joined, supporter retention has consistently been above industry standards—between 85 and 90 percent—with contributions growing steadily every year.

Relational Leader Concept	Identified
1. Worthy Intent	
2. Care About People's GPS	
3. Make Every Interaction Matter	
4. Value People Before Processes	
5. Connect Performance to a Purpose	
6. Intentionality	
7. Credibility	
8. Integrity	
9. Authenticity	
10. Business Performance	
Total Correct Answers	

Correct Responses: 1, 2, 5, 6, 10

3. BURNS ENGINEERING RELATIONSHIPS

Burns Engineering had done work with the Philadelphia International Airport and a few other clients for many years when Matt and John Burns succeeded their father at the helm of the firm. Despite the company's reputable presence in the infrastructure realm of Philadelphia engineering, Matt and John sought to expand the firm's clientele to include clients in transportation, education and beyond the Philadelphia region. To do this, they didn't just urge executives and supervisors to approach relationships more deliberately. Being an engineering firm, Burns naturally adopted a scientific process to achieve this goal. John Burns states,

"Being intentional about relationships using the Relational Capital process allows us to take an otherwise vague, soft-skill, emotional endeavor into a methodical process that can be measured over time. This is very helpful for technical people and us as we develop the future leaders of the firm."

Outside of the firm, the tools and processes help Burns Relational Leaders identify decision makers and influencers on projects so they can focus on uncovering Relational GPS and developing relationships with their clients. Then Burns professionals can work better collaboratively in teams to develop solutions for clients. Relational Capital techniques help to break down barriers that naturally form when dealing with a diverse group of stakeholders on a project.

Instead of seeing intentional relationships as a way to achieve goals, Burns views these relationships as goals themselves. Relationship competence is now a focused competency for all professionals in the Burns workplace. Candidates for employment are vetted on their relationship skills and new hires are trained to adhere to this process. John states, "Without some foundational relationship you can't extract their GPS, and without knowing their GPS you could unintentionally find them working against you."

It's tempting for companies in highly skilled disciplines to allow the technical proficiency of their work to speak for their Credibility and Integrity. While this is of course a large factor in earning a client's trust, Burns learned and has proved that it is only half the battle. Using a systematic method of experimentation, analysis and fine-tuning, Burns has set itself apart as a personable force in a very technical market. From a performance perspective Burns has grown revenues enough to double its payroll while also successfully integrating several acquisitions. Client feedback consistently results in strong satisfaction scores due in part to the firm's ongoing focus and development of strong business relationships.

Relational Leader Concept	Identified
1. Worthy Intent	
2. Care About People's GPS	
3. Make Every Interaction Matter	
4. Value People Before Processes	
5. Connect Performance to a Purpose	
6. Intentionality	
7. Credibility	
8. Integrity	
9. Authenticity	
10. Business Performance	
Total Correct Answers	

Correct Responses: 1, 4, 6, 7, 10

4. AMERISURE'S CHIEF RELATIONSHIP OFFICER

Amerisure is one of the nation's leading providers of commercial insurance. Its chief executive officer, Greg J. Crabb, announced to its select partner agencies that, after many in-depth discussions with them, it became clear he needed a role on his Executive Leadership Team that specifically focused on representing their voice in all key decisions. This role would be charged with leading the company's overall approach to its current and future relationships. With this in mind, Amerisure created the role of the chief relationship officer (CRO), filled by Todd Ruthruff.

In this role, Todd exemplifies a true CRO through every interaction and communication with its select partners. "As an agency-driven company that differentiates through superior service, it is critical that we are the best at understanding and responding to the needs and complexities of our agencies and policyholders. That can only be attained through our distinctive relationship approach that creates an exceptional customer experience." After this announcement, I had the opportunity to visit one of Amerisure's high-performing locations and witness this corporate-level commitment in action. This particular location is headed by Doug Roggenbaum and as Doug guided me through their offices, the first message I noticed read: *"We are focused on understanding and responding to the relationship, product and service needs of our existing and future Partners for Success agencies and their preferred customers."*

After I passed that sign, Doug explained that Amerisure does not work with just any insurance agency, but focuses and prioritizes working with a specific number of agencies so that they can provide the best possible experience for those agencies' customers. He went on to share how focused they were on their own internal relationships as well because if they are not operating effectively, customer results will miss the mark. Simultaneously, Amerisure also offers a formal relationship curriculum for their partner agencies as part of their branded PEAK Producer Program. Exclusive to Amerisure, this training was customized for the insurance industry to help its agents build impactful business relationships that create a sustainable competitive advantage. "Without relationships we're dealing with a commodity," said Jennifer DeMello-Johnson, Amerisure's AVP of Agency Services. "Competitor-proof relationships are the hardest thing to teach in our industry, and this program does exactly that."

Relational Leader Concept	Identified
1. Worthy Intent	
2. Care About People's GPS	
3. Make Every Interaction Matter	
4. Value People Before Processes	
5. Connect Performance to a Purpose	
6. Intentionality	
7. Credibility	
8. Integrity	
9. Authenticity	
10. Business Performance	
Total Correct Answers	

Correct Responses: 1, 3, 4, 6, 10

5. DISHWASHER TO THE BOARD ROOM
IN ONLY THIRTY YEARS

Way back when I was a twenty-year-old college student, I took a position as a dishwasher at the Jersey Shore. I always wanted to live and work "down the shore," as we say on the East Coast, and so did all of the other college kids. We took whatever jobs we could to pay rent for the three summer months. After a week (which seemed like a month) of doing dishes at a hotel restaurant, I moved out of the kitchen, gladly taking a busboy job. It was then that I met Larry, who owned the hotel and restaurant.

Larry was a great observer of human behavior and commented to me a few times about how many hours and double shifts I was working. He suggested I take a day off to enjoy the beach. I explained how I needed to save for my senior year of college and every hour mattered. I guess he noted this, because about a week later, a server position opened up and Larry chose me for the job. Better pay and hours meant I could actually go to the beach and some of the clubs at night. Things got even better a few weeks later, when a bartender left and I found myself behind the bar at one of the most lively outdoor bars in the beach town. My pay had doubled and the shift was even shorter. When summer ended, I headed back to college with cash and confidence that I could make it to the holidays before I would have to borrow from my parents or start working again.

Around October, I got a call in my dorm room from none other than Larry. He asked if I would like to meet up over the holidays to discuss my plans for the following summer. Of course, I agreed. Our meeting turned into him offering me the manager position at the hotel for the following summer. So in one summer, I went from a dishwasher to the manager. Now, *this* is where the story gets even better . . . As the hotel manager, I employed about sixty young people, one of whom was Larry's son, Kevin, who was sixteen and doing maintenance. I had many interactions with Kevin that I truly cannot remember, but somehow they made an impression. After I got a "real" job a few years later, I got a call from Kevin asking me for some advice on where to stay in the Philly area when he was visiting the University of Pennsylvania. I suggested he stay with my roommates and me. He did and he got into Penn, and then I didn't hear from him for almost thirty years.

When I next heard from Kevin thirty years later, he had become the chairman of his dad's company—Larry had owned the hotel as a hobby, believe it or not—and he asked me if I would like to visit. During our visit, he said he heard I had written a book and was interested in what it was all about. I explained it to him and the next thing I knew I was in front of his small board of directors.

Kevin explained that they all needed to get better at relationships and recounted the story of the time he stayed with me while visiting Penn. While I had actually forgotten about this, Kevin sure didn't. In fact, Kevin's company is a client today all because of how I managed the relationship a long time ago.

Relational Leader Concept	Identified
1. Worthy Intent	
2. Care About People's GPS	
3. Make Every Interaction Matter	
4. Value People Before Processes	
5. Connect Performance to a Purpose	
6. Intentionality	
7. Credibility	
8. Integrity	
9. Authenticity	
10. Business Performance	
Total Correct Answers	

Correct Responses: 1, 2, 3, 9, 10

INTERPRETATION

Total your correct answers (five per essay, with a maximum of 25). If you record 25 out of 25, you have completely internalized the most important Relational Leader concepts.

- 19–24: You have a strong grasp of the Relational Leader concepts.

- 13–18: Review the Relational Leader Insights at the end of Parts I and II and try the challenge again.

- 7–12: Peruse the first six chapters again prior to retaking the challenge.

- 0–7: Better read the book again.

13

FIVE WAYS TO SUSTAIN THE RELATIONSHIPS YOU CREATE

HAVING INVESTED SO MUCH time reinforcing existing relationships and establishing new ones, the last thing you want to do is see them evaporate. So here are five ways to keep you from falling into the trap of taking them for granted. While each of these approaches builds off the previous one, they can stand alone as well when applied to the relationships you create.

1. ALWAYS BE INTENTIONAL ABOUT RELATIONSHIPS

I shared during the introduction that a Relational Leader is anyone who *intentionally* puts the other person's goals and values at the forefront of each business relationship, creating an exceptional experience for others. This principle is known as Worthy Intent and it allows Relational Leaders to create relationships that immunize them against all competitors both within and outside their organizations. This resolve to act is the very first attribute that separates Relational Leaders from others. It must be present, evolve and remain evergreen in the Relational Leader's approach. Being intentional about business relationships is a career-long pursuit that allows the Relational Leader to launch, advance and elevate relationships across hierarchy and generations.

My challenge to you then is to make an intentional commitment to put the relationship at the forefront in all of your interactions.

2. BECOME GREAT AT OBSERVING BEHAVIORS

As Intentionality manifests, Relational Leaders become dialed in to the behaviors of the important business relationships and ad hoc, drive-by relationships around them. This capability can be developed whether you are an introvert or an extrovert; a Boomer, Gen or Millennial; a manager or a team member. It begins with paying attention through being completely in the moment with the person you are working with, then engaging them with well-thought-through questions and finally with capturing the Relational GPS that emerges from your discussion and utilizing that GPS to continue to build the relationship.

Therefore, by becoming a keen observer of your colleagues' behavior you will convey the thoughtfulness needed to create outstanding business relationships.

3. RESPECT AT-WILL RELATIONSHIPS

As I mentioned in chapter 1, most business structures today are a complex combination of hierarchical and cross-functional approaches. These structures are put into place to allow for more collaboration and innovation. However, they rely on subject matter experts from the hierarchy being available to support the cross-functional team work. The challenge is that compensation structures are not always geared toward these At-Will subject matter experts who are needed to support these efforts. Relational Leaders respect the role and challenges of their At-Will colleagues and find ways to adapt their approach to balance team and At-Will relationships, commitments and timelines. As a Relational Leader, seek to identify and advance your At-Will relationships in pursuit of your performance objectives.

4. POWER RELATIONAL CAPITAL THROUGH THE FIVE PRINCIPLES

Think of the best leaders you have observed and spent time with during your career. Now think about what made them memorable and great leaders in your eyes. You likely are recalling that their intentions were good, they stood for more than just the organization and they had a purpose that was bigger than themselves. The leader's common intention and focus in each example is on others and not themselves. This is where the Five Principles of the Relational Leader manifest to drive and transform leaders into Relational Leaders (figure 13-1).

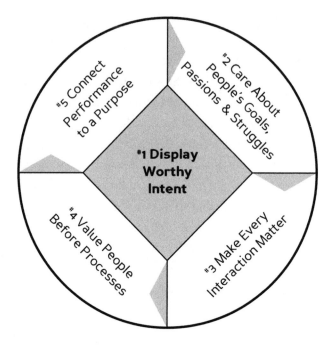

Figure 13-1. Relational Leadership.

As a Relational Leader your value proposition is to create a superior experience through the Five Principles for others as the key driver of business performance. By following these Five Principles, you will generate the power that fuels your success.

5. HARNESS YOUR RELATIONAL POWER

The power generated by the Five Principles then is harnessed through the Relational Agility Process, which enables Relational Leaders to bridge the generational gaps between Boomers, Gens and Millennials (figure 13-2); navigate the corporate maze; and collaborate with people to harness their collective talent, thought and effort.

#1 Display Worthy Intent			
#2 Care About People's Goals, Passions, & Struggles	#3 Make Every Interaction Matter	#4 Value People Before Processes	#5 Connect Performance to a Purpose
Advocate — Lead with Warmth; Focus on the Essential Qualities – Credibility, Integrity, Authenticity	Focus on using time purposefully with POP; Action Plan for all Important Business Relationships	Develop Personal Value Propositions; Apply Lateral and Vertical relationship strategies	**Develop Project Value Propositions; Career spanning Long Term investment in business relationship**
Professional Peer — Lead with Warmth; Focus on the Essential Qualities – Credibility, Integrity, Authenticity	Focus on using time purposefully with POP; Action Plan for all Important Business Relationships	**Develop Personal Value Propositions; Apply Lateral and Vertical relationship strategies**	
Colleague — **Lead with Warmth; Focus on the Essential Qualities – Credibility, Integrity, Authenticity**	**Focus on using time purposefully with POP; Action Plan for all Important Business Relationships**		

Increasing Value of Relational Capital

Figure 13-2. Relational Agility Process.

Relational Leaders who focus on harnessing the power they create through the Five Principles inspire a sense of purpose in those they work with. They see the larger good of the organization, the project or the product and the importance and excitement of their own role in supporting it. People perform at their best with a clear sense of purpose when challenged with the following five questions:

1. Who do I want to be?
2. How do I want to be perceived?

3. What am I here for?
4. What is most important to me?
5. What will my contribution be?

Ultimately, Relational Leaders amplify the Five Principles to connect with the people who power results, making performance a natural outcome as you are now connected to the true drivers of performance.

Championship coach Bill Parcells said one key to his success was to "reduce variables, improve performance." Relational Leaders leave nothing to chance when they focus on the relationships that will most impact their performance. Relational Leaders harness the power of Worthy Intent. They internalize and live the Five Principles that transform relationships into results. They capture hearts and exercise Relational Agility by influencing, collaborating and winning with people. Just as the performance in their organizations is a natural outcome so is their status as Relational Leaders. I challenge all of you to embrace the principles in this book and get *intentional* about developing Relational Capital and being a Relational Leader starting today. Life and work will be better and your team will thank you. I look forward to hearing about your success stories.

Relational Leaders' success comes through the experience they create for others.

APPENDIX

RELATIONAL LADDER ABSTRACT

Adapted from *Business Relationships That Last*,
Second edition, by Ed Wallace (Greenleaf, 2010)

HAVING A SENSE OF accomplishment in how we feel about our most important business relationships can also be very powerful and motivating. With this in mind, I created a list of activities that detail how to develop outstanding business relationships. I then applied all of my experiences with thousands of clients and partner relationships, along with research into client behaviors, to develop the Five Steps to Transform Contacts into High-Performing Business Relationships that follow:

1. Establish Common Ground: launch the relationship
2. Display Integrity and Trust: secure the relationship
3. Use Time Purposefully: invest in the relationship
4. Offer Help: share relational equity
5. Ask for Help: realize returns on your investment

In *Business Relationships That Last*, I explain each of these five steps in a way that will allow you to learn the new skills and processes that I promised earlier. You will also understand how the other key elements of Relational Capital—the principle of Worthy Intent, the essential qualities of Credibility, Integrity and Authenticity, and a client's Relational GPS—interact within these steps as you create and advance Relational Capital with your clients.

Visually, the five-step process can be represented by a ladder, which I call, appropriately enough, the Relational Ladder. Even though a ladder is very simple by design, it can be used to model increased levels of learning and skill development. You could think of a ladder as a metaphor for advancement, achievement, ascent and visibility in reaching a goal.

If you think of all your important business relationships as being somewhere on the ladder, you can then better determine which steps you need to take to advance these relationships at any given time. Each rung of the Relational Ladder represents a sequential step that moves you toward your most lasting professional relationships. Naturally, each time you move up a rung, you will feel encouraged that such a goal is attainable. Let me describe each part of the Relational Ladder in greater detail to anchor the image in your mind.

THE FRAME

Each side of the ladder's frame represents your specific skill sets. The right side of the Relational Ladder represents the hard skills, or the "science" of your business approach; the left side represents your soft skills, or the "art" of your business approach (see figure 14-1). We all have developed both to some extent throughout our careers: beginning with our first part-time jobs as teenagers, we then advanced these skills through higher education and work experience.

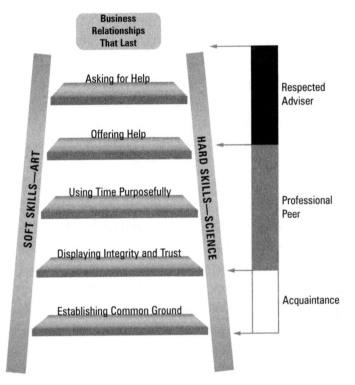

Figure A-1. The Relational Ladder.

Hard Skills: Science

The hard skills a client-facing professional needs in order to be successful include industry knowledge, product knowledge, ability to develop return on investment, technical abilities, sales metric proficiency and proposal-writing skills. Since most competing professionals can master these to a fairly effective degree, the science component in many careers has largely become an aspect of business that everyone is indistinguishably versed in.

Many client-facing professionals come to overly rely on their product-related hard skills when working with clients, which makes the ladder wobbly. We see this when client-facing professionals lead with every capability known to man during their initial discussions with their prospects without any sense as to what the prospect is trying to accomplish.

In fact, these capabilities are now expected—no, *required*—for client-facing professionals going into most business relationships. Therefore, emphasizing hard skills provides minimal opportunity for these professional men and women to distinguish themselves in the business relationship. However, there is an old saying that does bring the value of hard skills into perspective: "People do not care how much you know until they know how much you care."

One way you can distinguish yourself with a client is to select and adapt the parts of your technical competency and product knowledge that apply best to the specific business situation. Rather than playing back all of your knowledge about every feature and capability of your product and service, learn about specific client goals or passions or struggles to help you align specific elements of your offering to that client's Relational GPS.

People do not care how much you know until they know how much you care.

Soft Skills: Art

On the opposite side of the ladder frame are the soft skills, or the "art" of your business approach. Quite simply, these are your interpersonal skills and behaviors. Some of the soft skills required in business include friendliness, approachability, excellent verbal and written communication skills, listening, managing a network, presentation skills, negotiation and emotional intelligence. Many executives hire for these skills and assume that the client-facing professional can learn the complementary hard skills required to be successful in the new role. When soft skills are the only competency the professional can develop, however, this overemphasized side of the frame causes the ladder to become lopsided and unsteady as well.

We see this with client-facing professionals who believe that investing in continuous social entertaining is the key to unlocking a client's Relational GPS. The challenge with this approach is that in this commoditized world, most of their competitors have the capability to do the same, which results in this investment of time being no real point of distinction.

The Line Between Strengths and Weaknesses

The challenge we face is that we tend to gravitate toward the side of the ladder where we are strongest. Some of us, me included, exercise the soft skills more often, but if someone is best at exhibiting their hard skills, they will tend to emphasize those strengths. This tendency to *lean* toward where we are most comfortable—thus tipping the Relational Ladder—will eventually make us look to our clients like every other typical client-facing professional.

Picture yourself standing on a ladder. What is the main structural quality of the ladder that you are depending on to keep it from falling to one side or the other? The answer is balance! Developing outstanding business relationships involves carefully balancing science and art, a combination of your hard and soft skills. Neither of these two components should greatly outweigh the other. Think, for example, about the effect of spending all of your time with clients entertaining them instead of talking about business. On the other hand, always talking about technical specifications but never really listening to the client or relaxing enough to get to know him on a more personal level can be just as ineffective.

The Rungs

Now that we can visualize our hard and soft skills as the framework for supporting every one of our business relationships, we can think of each of the rungs as one of the steps in the Five Steps to

Transform Contacts into High-Performing Relationships. These steps are the true secrets to success in any business relationship. Applying what you learn from each of these steps will help you identify, measure and proactively improve how you relate to your most important business relationships.

So when we place the five steps—establishing common ground, displaying Integrity and trust, using time purposefully, offering help and asking for help—onto the Relational Ladder, you will see how each element has a special role to play in moving you upward from one step to the next:

- Your ability to launch a relationship and move off of the first rung depends on building Credibility, becoming believable so your clients will share their Relational GPS with you.
- Your Integrity emerges when you deliver on your commitments to your clients time and time again.
- Your ability to reach the top rung of the Relational Ladder depends on creating sufficient Relational Capital with your client by reflecting your Worthy Intent throughout the process to the point where they begin to ask for your point of view—even on issues outside of your business together.

Realizing that there is an underlying process that orders the apparent randomness of business relationships is your first step toward gaining—and sustaining—relational fluency.

ENDNOTES

CHAPTER 1. The Relationship Paradox

1. Candice Bennett and Associates in "A Better Way to Measure and Value Business Relationships," Relational Capital Group (April 2010): www.relationalcapitalgroup.com/downloads/EnterpriseRQ-whitepaper.pdf.

2. David Bush and Chris Malone, "Resolving Cross-Functional Collaboration Challenges," The Relational Capital Group (May 2012): www.relationalcapitalgroup.com/downloads/Cross-Functional-Collaboration-White-Paper.pdf.

3. RQ Assessment, Relational Capital Group, data from 2008–2015; Business Relationship Study: Candice Bennett and Associates (2010).

CHAPTER 2. Principle #1: Display Worthy Intent

1. Susan T. Fiske, Amy J. C. Cuddy and Peter Glick, "Universal Dimensions of Social Cognition: Warmth and Competence," *Trends in Cognitive Sciences* 11, no. 2 (2006): 77–83.

CHAPTER 8. Launching Business Relationships with Colleagues

1. Aubrey Daniels, "What It Really Takes to Manage a Multi-Generational Workforce," Tracom Group (October 6, 2015): www.tracomcorp.com/blog/what-it-really-takes-to-manage-a-multi-generational-workforce/

GLOSSARY

Advocate—person with whom you have a career-spanning business relationship that goes beyond the scope of the common goals that you have worked on over the years

At-Will Relationships—discretionary relationships that are needed to accomplish objectives; business relationships that require Relational Capital investment due to a lack of connection to common performance objectives

Authenticity—the state of being genuine; being yourself

Capability—the ability to do something

Collaborate—work together on something in common

Colleague—businesspeople who know each other or simply acknowledge they work for the same organization, but have not worked on common goals previously

Competence—the improved version of "capability"; advanced degree of skill

Credibility—the power to elicit belief

Dimensionality—strategic levels in the Relational Agility Process that Relational Leaders intentionally decide to launch, advance or elevate their important business relationships to

Important Business Relationships (IBRs)—term used to describe relationships that Relational Leaders prioritize based on their goals

Integrity—adherence to ethical standards; honesty

Intentionality—the means that Relational Leaders collaborate through a principled, purposeful and practical relational approach

Lateral and Vertical Relationship Planning—process where Relational Leaders identify existing and At-Will important business relationships

Personal Value Proposition—taking a value proposition and personalizing it with a story or anecdote that supports the value proposition

Professional Peer—work together as peers despite role/hierarchy in the business relationship

Project Value Proposition—specific value proposition developed to take the project or opportunity to a level that connects performance to a purpose

POP—acronym that represents purpose, outcomes and process: three steps for planning effective meetings

Relational Agility—capability to apply the Five Principles to collaborate effectively with Colleagues, Professional Peers and Advocates leading to superior performance

Relational Agility Process—a process that Relational Leaders use to fluidly conduct collaborative interactions so that they create Relational Capital with Colleagues, Professional Peers and Advocates

Relational Attributes—positive traits we attach to people we like to work with

Relational Capital—the value created by people in a business relationship

Relational GPS—the road map or shorthand for every business relationship. Focus is on the other person's business or personal goals, causes or passions, and business or personal struggles

Relational Leader—anyone who intentionally harnesses the power of Worthy Intent to create an exceptional experience for other people

Relational Micro-moments—discrete relational opportunities to learn about the other person's Relational GPS or just to help them have a better day

Relational Strategy—intentional approach to launching, advancing or elevating relationships with Colleagues, Professional Peers and Advocates

Relationship—when people share something in common

Relationship Management—a strategic process whereby a company intentionally prioritizes, measures and advances its most important business relationships aligned with its performance objectives

Receptive Will—the attribute of being open to another person's outreach and nonjudgmental around the purpose for that outreach

Sources of Value—attributes that people recognize when working with a Relational Leader

Value Proposition—a clear statement, through the eyes of the other party, that provides some kind of benefit

Warmth and Competence—research-based approach that indicates humans respond positively more often when approached with warm versus competent gestures

Worthy Intent—the inherent promise you make to put the other person's best interest at the core of your business relationship

INDEX

acquisitions, failure, 3, 155

action planning, 134–135

Advocates, 107, 108, 113, 162, 205
  business relationship dimension
    breakout, 159–160
  elevating relationships with,
    151–160
  in Relational Agility Process, 111,
    151

Affordable Care Act (ACA), 92

agenda, for meetings, 131–133

Amerisure, chief relationship officer,
  184–186

Armstrong, David, 32

art (soft skills), in Relational Ladder,
  200–201

assessment of others, 34–36

At-Will relationships, 16–17, 99, 105,
  205
  care for, 149
  generations, 111
  respect for, 193

Authenticity, 64–67, 205
  indicators, 66

Baby Boomers, 110–111
  in org model complexity, 23
  Relational GPS for connecting
    with, 53

Barkann, Michael, 180

Barkann family Healing Hearts
  Foundation, 180–182

Barnes, Mike, 181

behaviors
  ability to assess, 45–46
  assessment and, 166
  observable for Relational Leaders,
    171–172
  observing, 192
  science of, 124

belief
  for competitor-proof relation-
    ships, 25–26
  inspiring, 1

Boomers, see Baby Boomers

brands, customer relationships, 1

Burns, John, 182–183

Burns Engineering relationships,
  182–184

Bush, David, 166

business, margin for error in, 27–30

business relationships, 11–13, 107
  assessment for Advocate, 152
  beginning, 54
  with Colleagues, 119–135
  common goals in, 44–45
  compromise of, 158
  contacts transformed into

high-performing, 197
dimension breakout, 159–160
Relational Ladder for advancing, 103–105
see also important business relationships (IBRs)
Business Relationships That Last, 197–202
business structure, hierarchical, 24

cable company
changing process for customer, 87–88
customer service, 82–84
capability, 205
Carteaux, Bill, 76
chief relationship officer, of Amerisure, 184–186
Children's Hospital of Philadelphia (CHOP), xvii–xix, 37
Coates, Frank, 108
collaborate, 105–106, 205
collaboration
vs. command and control, 25
cross-functional, 20
goals and, 113–114
Colleagues, 106, 108, 111, 205
business relationship dimension breakout, 159–160
business relationships with, 119–135
guidelines for launching relationships, 123
commitment, 62
to helping others, 91
communication
electronic, 75, 175
handwritten notes, 175

town hall meetings for, 178–180
see also meetings
competence, 34–38, 205, 207
connection, 29
relationships to goals, 115–117
core values, 86
Crabb, Greg J., 184
Credibility, 58–59, 183, 205
indicators, 61
Relational Ladder and, 202
cross-functional collaboration, 20
cross-generational relationships, 53
Customer Relationship Management (CRM), 12
customer relationships, impact, 18
customer service, cable company, 82–84
customers
as company priority, 85–87
listening to, 86

Daniels, Aubrey, 124
DaVita, 90–93
Village Service Day, 92–93
DeMello-Johnson, Jennifer, 185
DiBonaventure, Lynn, 22–24
Dimensionality, 106–109, 161, 205
disciplines, 86
discontinuous innovation, 54
discretionary relationships, 16
see also At-Will relationships
dishwasher to board room promotions, 186–188
documenting short-term objectives, 51

EffectiveMeetings.com, 126–127
electronic communications, 75
vs. handwritten notes, 175

employees
    as company priority, 85–87
    town hall meetings with, 178–180
energy, negative, 157
Enterprise Relationships, 18–21
ethereal relationships, 50
Executive Summary, 98–99, 161–162

Facebook, 50
face-to-face communications, 75
family health emergency, xvii–xviii
Feeney, Tom, 1, 85–86
Fiske, Dr., 34
friending, 50
functional group research, 18–21

gap analysis, lateral and vertical,
    170–171
generational formula, 28
generations, 110–111
    alignment, 124–125
    bridging gaps, 5
Gens, 110, 111
    in org model complexity, 23
    Relational GPS for connecting
        with, 53
global positioning systems (GPS),
    55
    see also Relational GPS
goals
    collaboration and, 113–114
    connecting to relationships,
        115–117
    determining, 115
    dimensions of accomplishing, 109
    table to record, 166–167
goals of others, 56
    caring about, 49–69, 120, 125
    connecting relationships to, 113

personalization, 143
    as priorities, 43
Golden Gate Bridge, toll taker on,
    72
golf caddies, golf shot strategy con-
    versation, 46
golf driving range, 39–41, 45
grassroots workers, meetings with,
    179
Great Places to Work Institute, 63
groups of people, 110–111
    functional research, 18–21

handwritten notes, 175
hard skills, in Relational Ladder,
    199–200
Hicks, Cam, 52
hierarchical business structure, 24
hiring process, 91
human factor, and initiative failure,
    32
human relationships, see relation-
    ships

important business relationships
    (IBRs), 115–116, 205
    identifying, 146
    information tracking on, 125
    recording, 146
information age, 27
innovation, discontinuous, 54
Integrity, 61–64, 183, 206
    indicators, 63
    Relational Ladder and, 202
Intentionality, 5, 13–16, 27, 206
    about relationships, 191–192
    behaviors validating, 44
    plans and strategies in, 165
    steps in, 114–117, 161

intentions of others, determining, 34

interactions
significance of each, 71–79
and time use, 126–128

introductions, 149–150, 162

investments, executive committee approval for, 154–156

James, LeBron, 21
judging others, 34–36

lateral and vertical relationship
planning, 144–149, 206
requirements, 147–149
templates, 170–171
leadership, 32
best practice, 51
power of, 25–30
role of, 1
LinkedIn, 50
listening, practicing, 59

Main Line Animal Rescue (MLAR), 94–96
Malone, Chris, 34, 37
matrix-based organization, 106
measuring, relationship strength, 166–171
meetings, 126–128
conducting impactful, 172–174
outcomes of, 129–130
POP approach, 128–135, 162
process (agenda) for, 131–133
purpose of, 128–129
schedule for, 133
town hall, 178–180
mergers and acquisitions, success or failure, 3, 155

Micro-moments, Relational, 27, 72–75, 98, 207
branding, 73–75
Millennials, 110, 111
in org model complexity, 23
Relational GPS for connecting with, 53
"mission-driven hearts," 91
mutual relationships, and Receptive Will, 156

negative energy, 157
new products
Relational Leadership for, 178–180
relationships and integration, 138
notes, handwritten, 175

objectives, documenting short-term, 51
office environment, 78
one-to-one relationships, 29–30, 113–114
Operation Clean Sweep, 77
org chart, 14–16
Organization 1.0, 23
Organization 2.0, 24, 110
Organization 3.0, 32, 62–63, 85
one-to-one relationships, 29–30, 113–114
organizational dynamics, 23
organizations, 3–4
matrix-based, 106
others
assessment of, 34–36
commitment to helping, 91
determining intentions, 34
see also goals of others
outcomes, of meetings, 129–130, 173

paid time off (PTO), unlimited, 78
paradigm shift, for Safelite leaders,
    1–2
Parcells, Bill, 196
passions, 56
    caring about others', 120, 125
patents, as intangible asset, 3–4
PEAK Producer Program, curricu-
    lum for partner agencies, 185
peer relationships, impact, 18
penmanship, 175–176
people
    as problem with process, 84–88
    types of, 22–24
    valuing before processes, 81–88,
        139–144
performance, 78
    connecting to purpose, 89–99,
        151–152
    town hall meetings and, 179–180
personal value proposition, 140–144,
    174, 206
planning
    action, 134–135
    lateral and vertical relationship,
        144–149
    Work Planning and Review Sys-
        tem (WPRS), 50–52
    see also Relational Agility Action
        Planner
Plastic Industry Association, 76–78
POP (purpose, outcomes, process)
    for meetings, 128–135, 162,
        172–174, 206
    sample, 131–132
power, for Relational Agility Process,
    194–196
practice
    of listening, 59

need for, 21
    with purpose, 39–41
printing, 3-D, 77
priorities, xviii–xix
    goals and values of others as, 2–3,
        43
    managers discussion with em-
        ployees, 51
    shareholders, customers, or em-
        ployees, 85–87
processes
    for meetings, 131–133, 174
    people as problem, 84–88
    people valued before, 81–88,
        139–144
    relationship gaps between boxes,
        145–146
productive relationships, 20
productivity, organizational structure
    impact, 29
Professional Peers, 107, 108, 111, 206
    business relationship dimension
        breakout, 159–160
    relationships with, 137–150
profits, vs. purpose, 93
progress conversations, building rela-
    tionships through, 50–52
project value proposition, 154–156,
    206
promises, keeping, 62
proximity dilemma, 75–79
puppy mill abuse, 95
purpose
    connecting performance to,
        151–152
    of meetings, 128–129, 173
    vs. profits, 93

quality, 105

Receptive Will, 158, 162, 207
and overcoming distractors,
156–157
recognition, 51–52
recycling, 76–77
referrals, 149, 162
Relational Agility, 5, 6, 206
Relational Agility Action Planner,
143–144, 168–169
for Advocates, 153
for Colleague, 133–134
completed, 160
Relational Agility Process, 103–117,
137, 206
for Advocates, 151
dimensions, 107
executive summary, 161–162
power for, 194–196
summary, 159–160
table, 111
Relational Attributes, 12, 206
Relational Capital, 78, 84, 143, 206
building value, 67–69
definition, 2, 98
increasing, 113
Intentionality and, 27
principles of, 193–194
qualities, 121–122
Relational GPS and, 69
Relational Ladder and, 202
Relational GPS, 53–69, 98, 207
capturing, 56–59
focus on uncovering, 183
Relational Ladder, 103
abstract, 197–202
frame, 198–202
hard skills (science), 199–200
rungs, 201–202
soft skills (art), 200–201

Relational Leader Challenge, 177–
189
Amerisure's chief relationship officer, 184–186
Barkann family Healing Hearts
Foundation, 180–182
Burns Engineering relationships,
182–184
for new products, 178–180
promotions, 186–188
Relational Leadership, 2–3, 207
actions by, 157–158
insights, 98–99
observable behaviors for, 171–172
principles of, 5–7
relationship environment of, 105
Relational Micro-moments, 27,
72–75, 98, 207
branding, 73–75
Relational Strategy, 207
relational superiority complex, 21–22
relationship development
accidental, 4
identifiable principles for effective, 4–5
Relationship Intentionality, process
design and, 22
Relationship Leaders, need for, 25
Relationship Management, 207
Relationship Paradox, 11–30
confirmation of, 20
relationships, 207
complexity, 147
connecting to goals, 115–117
cross-generational, 53
difficulty in, 11
lateral and vertical planning,
144–149
measuring strength, 166–171

mutual, and Receptive Will, 156
with Professional Peers, 137–150
and success, 3–5, 31
sustaining, 191–196
transformative, 75
universal framework for, 52–69
see also business relationships;
    important business relation-
    ships (IBRs)
research, functional group, 18–21
retail salesperson, warmth in ap-
    proach, 38
risk to project, 147
Robinson, Lynn, 91
Roggenbaum, Doug, 185
Romer, John, 91
RQ Assessment, 21, 22, 166, 167
Ruthruff, Todd, 184

Safelite AutoGlass, 1
    priorities, 85–87
science (hard skills), in Relational
    Ladder, 199–200
SEA Research Foundation, 77
self-focus, 49–50
senior executives, on relationships
    and success, 12
shareholder/board relationships, im-
    pact, 18
shareholders, as company priority,
    85–87
short-term objectives, documenting,
    51
Smith, Benson, 50
Smith, Bill, 94–96
soft skills (art), in Relational Ladder,
    200–201
sources of value, 207
    worksheet, 142, 174

Southwest Airlines, 73–75
strategic alliances, 16
strength of relationships, measuring,
    166–171
strengths and weaknesses, balance in
    Relational Ladder, 201
struggles, 56
    caring about others', 120, 125
subject matter experts, 17
success, 53
    and human relationships, 3–5
    relationships and, 12, 19, 31
supplier relationships, impact, 18
synapses, 24, 105, 147

takeaways, from meetings, 129–130
team relationship gap analysis tem-
    plate, 148
technical competency, 199–200
technology, promise of, 20
Teleflex, 50–52
thinking between the boxes,
    145–146
thoughtfulness, making other's goals
    as priority, 44–45
3-D printing, 77
time
    meeting scheduling, 133
    wasting in meetings, 127
Tommy Boy (movie), 119–121
tools
    lateral and vertical relationship
        templates, 170–171
    Relational Agility Action Planner,
        168–169
    sources of value worksheet, 142,
        174
town hall meetings, 178–180
transformative relationships, 75

trust, 52, 98
building, 63
as Worthy Intent consequence, 33–34, 47
Tuttle, Tyler, 92
Twitter, 50

value propositions, 140–141, 162, 207
for project, 154–156

warmth and competence, 34–38, 207
testing, 60–61
weaknesses and strengths, balance in Relational Ladder, 201
website, instructions for RQ calculation, 167

Whole Foods Markets, 95
work flow, org chart and, 15
Work Planning and Review System (WPRS), 50–52
Worthy Intent, 3, 36, 98, 191–192, 207
absence of, 156
believing and sharing, 60
benefits of displaying, 47
definition, 33
displaying, 31–47, 121
focus on power of, 96
power of, xvii–xix, 196
Relational Agility Process and, 112
trust as consequence, 33–34

OTHER BOOKS BY ED WALLACE

Fares to Friends: How to Develop Outstanding Business Relationships, Ed Wallace (RCG Press, 2006)

Creating Relational Capital, John Holland and Ed Wallace (RCG Press, 2008)

Business Relationships That Last: 5 Steps that Transform Contacts into High-Performing Relationships, Ed Wallace (Greenleaf Book Group, 2010; updated edition 2014)